Is It Safe to Friend a
Dead Guy On Facebook?

Steve Krupnik

Illustrated by
Joe M Ruiz

www.deadguyonfacebook.com

#DGOFB

Copyright © 2014 Steve Krupnik
All rights reserved
Published in the United States of America by Cloud Ten Inc.
808 Trail Ridge East
Mishawaka, IN 46544

Visit www.deadguyonfacebook.com for
additional copies and further updates

ISBN-10: 0692021957
ISBN-13: 9780692021958

Illustrations by Joe M. Ruiz

www.studiourge.com

*This book is for my wife, Velma. She's my rock.
Without her nothing else really matters.*

Contents

Introduction	7
How This Book Came About	11
Smartphone Junkies	16
Social Media Junkies	50
Video Game Junkies	78
Texting Junkies	91
Conclusion	109
Author Biography	115

Introduction

Several years ago I made the decision to switch careers. I wound up selling two active and profitable businesses to do what I do today. Nowadays when people ask what I do for a living, I condense my answer considerably to avoid confusion or boredom. What do I tell them I do? I write. An amusing answer considering my high school English teacher would laugh herself to tears at even the thought I would ever be a writer. Well, I am.

What do I write? Mostly information products for niche industries specifically about their business. You've seen this stuff before: workbooks, audio CD courses, coaching programs, informational DVDs, newsletters—that sort of thing. I also write copy for marketing and advertising. I have a book out there regarding one specific niche industry, and I also write frequent e-mail tips that go out weekly to people in this industry who choose to receive them. All this writing challenges me greatly to keep my creative energy flowing—the exact reason I chose to do what I do. Yet I did not choose to write the book you are holding in your hand. I believe it chose me, and I hope you find it fun and entertaining. It's my goal to provide you some fodder for laughter and also for a good dose of reality. Maybe not your reality but certainly mine.

I wrote this book solely based on my observations of the world around me. I did not write this book to upset or insult anyone, but I can guarantee it will upset a few readers. If one of them turns out to be you, I refuse to apologize. Because if at any time in reading these words you begin to feel pissed off, stupid, insulted, or assaulted, it's not my fault. The fault is solely yours. It's your reaction to the stories I'm telling in this book. But if your reaction causes you to stop and think about how you choose to live your life, it will prove to be a good and useful thing. Thinking is always a good thing and is growing exceedingly rare, so if this book makes you think, I believe I've accomplished my purpose in writing it. It's a book I've always wanted to write but just never knew it.

This book is about a tragic epidemic going on around us. That dreadful disconnect between human beings and the real world they live in. This book is about a frightful lack of attention these human beings pay to the people and things surrounding them. It's about a self-induced attention deficit disorder brought on by a serious addiction to the digital devices they choose to surround themselves with. Because of this I predict there will be two distinctly different types of readers of this book. Which will you be?

The first type of readers will not find this book to be funny at all. But they may consider it to be a good dose of reality, because in reading it they will realize they have turned themselves into digital junkies. Addicts. Cyber slaves to their devices. They may also wake up to the fact that their devices are no longer an asset but a liability in their lives. A cyber time suck, a digital rabbit hole, disconnecting their brains from the real world around them. If you discover you are this first type of reader, I have a warning for you. You may find yourself angry with me over the content in this book. You may even try to contact me through the book's website at Deadguyonfacebook.com. Don't bother as you will be wasting even more time. This is because I really do not care.

Quite frankly, it's none of my business how you choose to live your life. And if you choose to live your life as an out-of-touch digital junkie, it makes absolutely no sense to try and justify your disjointed lifestyle to me. Again, it's not my deal; it's yours. You are free to live your life any way you choose.

The second type of readers will have a completely different reaction to the contents of this book. They will frequently find themselves shaking their heads and saying, *Man you've got that one right, Steve.* Occasionally they may even have to put the book down for a few minutes just to catch their breath and wrap their brain around the content. Some may even need to keep a tissue handy to wipe away the tears of laughter they experience from the sidesplitting reality of it all. In reading this book, if you discover you are solidly in this second category, I would like to ask a couple things of you.

First, each and every one of us knows at least one digital junkie. You may know several, or maybe your entire circle of friends and acquaintances qualify. What I ask you to do is share the contents of this book with them. I wouldn't, however, suggest you buy them a copy and beg them to read it. This would prove to be a complete waste of your time and money. That's because you cannot reach these people through conventional means like buying them the book as a gift. The only way you can reach them is through their devices, and I've made it easy for you to do so on the book's website at Deadguyonfacebook.com. Have at it, and have fun with it.

The second thing I'm requesting of you is on a more serious note. You may well know a digital junkie who is also a loved one: a family member, a best friend, a spouse, or a child. And the possibility of this is getting greater every day. What I'm asking you to do is call your loved one out on it. Gently. Have a kind and caring talk with this person regarding his or her digital addiction. We find ourselves living in some very interesting and, at least occasionally, trying times. Getting through some of these times safely and securely requires a good deal of mental and spiritual strength. You do not, however, build your mental and spiritual strength without a solid connection to the world around you and also the world above you.

It's been my experience that the people in this world with the least amount of mental and spiritual strength also happened to be digital junkies. Coincidence? I don't think so. As a matter fact, I'll prove it to you in this book. And if you experience any successes in calling out your loved ones on their addiction, I would love to hear from you. Fair enough? Do them this favor, and you will end up helping us all.

    I truly hope you get a good dose of enjoyment and benefit from my story. Thank you.

How This Book Came About

It's Tuesday morning, and I'm in my office chair writing my ass off. That's what I do. I'm an author, publisher, and business coach. The coffee cup is dry, and my stomach is beginning to growl. OK, another cup of coffee. I haven't quite reached the end of my time blocked for this writing assignment, so the tummy is going to have to wait. Noon comes quickly, and the writing project has finished its second edit. Click, save, close.

Time for a spot of lunch and a quick review of today's e-mail. On my third bite of the barbecued beef brisket, I spot one of those annoying e-mails from Facebook wanting me to connect with additional people on the site. I rarely go to the website. I know very little about it actually. But my Webmaster, Wally the Webguy, set it up so I would have a Facebook page and all the stuff that I write for websites and blogs and other materials automatically drops onto my Facebook page. At least it is supposed to. The Webmaster told me it was a wise thing to do. I have other thoughts. When I do occasionally go to the site just to make sure the automation thing is still working, I can't help but note the ridiculous amount of psychobabble mindlessly posted on the site by people I don't even know and a few I'm somewhat familiar with. Doesn't matter to me. I couldn't care less what Facebook game they are currently playing. Just don't ask me to participate.

So I open the e-mail from Facebook, expecting to quickly delete it, but something catches my attention under the headline "people you may know." It's an avatar of a guy I actually do know, and Facebook wants me to friend him on its website. All right, social media site, I know the guy. Obviously better than you do. I happen to know that he's dead. Do you really want me to friend him at this stage of the game? Kind of creepy. Heck, I've had numerous adult beverages and conversations with this guy. What have you done for him, Facebook? And why didn't you ask me to friend him when he was still upright and breathing? Did you wait on purpose? Is this nothing more than a cruel techie joke?

And what if I did friend him now that he's room temperature? Is that safe? Will his cyber spirit decide to possess my Facebook page and turn it into some sort of zombie? Nah, he wasn't that kind of guy. He was a good, thoughtful spirit even though he was a recovering attorney. He may have questioned my sanity about writing this book though. So what's wrong with having a Facebook page after you have moved on from this world? What's wrong with having someone *friend* you after you've gone on to the other side? Isn't it like a digital diary immortalizing what you did in your cyber life? Not only no, but hell no.

Of course, I say this for a very specific reason. It's been my observation that many people treat Facebook as more than just a social media website. I don't know why, but at least in my world, when people on the website choose to share something about what's going on in their lives, they come across looking like assholes. That's nice, I'm dead now, and the world will always remember what an asshole I was. My assholiness is now immortal thanks to Facebook. Usually when you die, the people who knew you try to remember all the good stuff you did in your life. Yet one stupid drunk post on the Facebook website can change all of that for you. People generally have very short memories. Facebook pages do not. And I can't for the life of me figure out why people do this to themselves.

They share the damnedest things in a permanent public forum. Think I'm kidding? As I'm writing this, I just hit the Facebook website, and what's the first thing I see? Some asshole that I don't even know took a picture of his lunch and posted it on Facebook before he ate it. He even described exactly what the plate contained. Now who in the hell would ever, and I mean ever, be interested in what this guy is eating for lunch? Are you kidding me? OK, by the looks of his lunch, his cardiac surgeon might be interested in what he's shoving in his pie hole. *Save me some space in the OR because it looks like my patient Peter may be coming in really soon for a quadruple bypass.* Or maybe after Peter passes, his friends and family can review the Facebook pictures of his luncheons in horror and grief over what exactly took him to meet his maker. Has Peter no pride? Obviously not.

He is treating his body like a garbage dumpster and choosing to record it in perpetuity.

Then there are the annoying bastards that treat the Facebook website as a platform to foist their political viewpoints on anyone unfortunate enough to read any of their posts. It does not matter whether it's some bleeding heart liberal wanting to spend the world into a permanent state of bankruptcy or some ultraconservative hell bent on erasing several hundred years of political corruption in an attempt to take us back to a so-called better time. I don't care. For these poor souls, I have one very simple message. Plain and simple, your political points of view are absolutely none of my business. Your feeble attempts to sell me on your style of politics will never sway my personal feelings one iota. Take your agendas and shove them up your asses. If you really want to fix the political mess we're all in, become a little more active in your community and a whole hell of a lot less active on Facebook. Get it? Every morning when I first wake up, I thank God I do not get as much government as I pay for. That's it.

And how about the politicians and political pundits all spewing out their sociopathic points of view on Facebook for all to see?

Here's the key to this one; take a look and see what these types are usually posting to Facebook. You can't help but discover that their brilliance is nothing more than posting other politician and political pundit types' crap up there to try and make opposing political points of view look even sillier than theirs. Now that's productive. Don't any of these types ever take a stab at thinking for themselves? Apparently not. *If you agree with my political psychopathic point of view, I'll make you look like a hero on my Facebook page. And if you disagree, I'll do my best to post your worst stuff to make you appear to be the village idiot that you are.* That's productive. What the hell ever happened to sitting down and having an adult discussion on our important political decisions and the issues we face that we may disagree on? Oh, I digress, politicians and political pundits on Facebook wouldn't recognize an adult conversation if it walked up to them and tapped them on the shoulder. Lord help us all.

I understand there may be some enjoyment to following your favorite politicians on their Facebook pages. I'm sure there is for them as they can lie to you in real time. It becomes quite obvious when viewing their pages that they couldn't care less about their lies becoming a permanent part of their Facebook page. When they are not lying to you on their Facebook pages, the second most popular activity is finger-pointing. *It's his fault, it's her fault, it's this party's fault, it's that party's fault,* and never do any of them suggest anything of substance to work together as a government team. Nor do they ever admit that the ridiculous things going on in government and all of the unproductive gridlock may actually be at least partially their fault. It's much healthier on their next campaign to instead just blame the other guy.

Of course, there are some politicians who attempt to put their personal lives on their Facebook pages to make themselves appear more human and less politician. They share things like their bios; their families; their personal hobbies; and in the case of Anthony Weiner, their penises. Anthony, you lovable piece of man candy.

Who knew you could go to a social media site and get a glimpse of Weiner's wiener? For that matter who cares? You don't even need to be a well-known politician to get considerable play from doing some very questionable activities on your Facebook page.

In the town where I reside, South Bend, Indiana, the community and the local media have been really abusing a city councilman for the past couple months. He posted an extremely graphic picture on his Facebook page of a naked man with his dog. Well, I don't really follow the local news, and all I can tell you is the thing has drug out endlessly, and not only is the city council involved but so is the city attorney, the state police, and also numerous citizens filing complaints with various agencies. Seriously, if you live in South Bend, you simply cannot get away from this story. Did the city councilman make a mistake posting this picture to his Facebook page? Of course he did. Did he at least have good intentions for doing what he did? Who knows? The story accompanying the photograph may have been something he felt was important, and he wanted the opinions of his constituents. Or maybe a few too many martinis caused a moment of poor judgment? It doesn't matter. I bring this up because it's amazing what a big deal so many people can make out of a moment of bad thinking on a social media site. Leave the guy alone, and go investigate something that will make our community a better place to live. And if you still want to rough this guy up, why don't you grow a pair and run against him in the next election.

OK, back to the book. So who do we pick on first? I've got to go with the one I personally find the most annoying. Smartphone junkies.

Smartphone Junkies

On occasion I feel a bit vintage when my kid can't wait to show me the latest app on her iPhone, and I laugh telling her I used to own a bag phone and a brick phone. My comment quickly brings on her young deer-in-the-headlights stare.

"A what?"

"Never mind. It doesn't matter."

I do however mention to her, on occasion, that it may be wise for her to give herself a reality check to make sure she is still smarter than her telephone device. At least she would have to use her brain in order to do so. A good thing I think, pun intended.

Understand that I fully realize, after being in business for my entire adult life, what a convenience it is and how profitable it can be to own a cell phone. As I told you, I got in during the early bag phone years—if you're old enough to remember what the hell they were. Kind of like a man purse that you would occasionally answer. And I actually liked my brick phone. It looked kind of manly. The reception was far better than the bag phone. By the way, if you are unaware of what these things were, they were called brick phones because they were literally the size, shape, and weight of a real brick. Not only was it a pretty good communication device, but it could also double as a self-defense weapon. Pretty cool.

But just because I had those things early on does not truly indicate I'm any kind of a technical guy. I keep my cell phones until it's absolutely impossible to find batteries for the model I'm carrying. Then I live out the same scenario, going down to the plan provider, having some pimple-faced, hormone-raging, ADHD teenage boy asking what he can do for me. And what does he say when I pull out my phone? "You're not still carrying one of those, are you?" Thanks, kid. But in the past twenty years or so, these highly infrequent trips to my cell phone provider have gotten far more complicated.

Now, the conversation might go something like this:

Yes, I am still carrying one of those. But I've scoured the earth, and batteries for this model are no longer available. Looks like I need a new phone.

Well, sir, what would you like your new phone to do?

Young man, I would like my new phone to be capable of placing calls, remembering my contacts, taking calls, and sending a vast majority of those calls to voice mail. I also need it to have Bluetooth capabilities. Any questions?

That last requirement is a new one for me and makes me feel I'm at least a bit technical. Didn't think I'd use it, but I really dig the hands-free thing built into my car and use it all the time, returning calls as I drive.

Come on, it's hands-free. I'm no baby killer when I'm talking on my cell phone with both hands on the wheel and my eyes on the road. At least I don't have a beer between my legs. Besides, I never answer my cell phone when it rings, and, yes, mine still rings, unless it's my wife or kid. So I usually have voice mails to return at my convenience. The only time in my mind that it's convenient to do so is when I'm driving from point A to point B. Justified easily by me to be a very good use of my time.

So when I get done telling the kid what I want my new cell phone to do, that's when the barrage of questions starts. Do you text? No. You stream any music? No. Maybe a built-in GPS? No. Internet access? No. Pictures and video? No. After he covers maybe twenty features or so, most of them I have no idea what he's talking about, I subtly but firmly remind him again: "Make calls, remember my contacts, answer calls, send them to voice mail, and Bluetooth. That's it. Get it?"

Then he always gives me a look like I'm using a Dixie cup and a string or something. Don't get in a shooting match of wit with me, kid, or it will quickly be obvious you have no ammunition. It's my personal choice on what type of cell phone I wish to carry, and it would also be my personal choice to kick your ass if you give me too much grief in doing so. Don't make me come over there.

As a kid I had great hope of how new technologies would improve my life as I moved through adulthood. And many of them have. I used to dig watching Captain James T. Kirk on Star Trek, back when it was just a television show, with all the cool electronic gadgets the good captain had at his disposal. The mobile communication device—cool stuff, and now it's a reality. The phaser—one handy self-defense gadget. Thanks, Captain, I now own a very similar device.

And how about the transporter room? Way cool and not here yet, but I sure would like to own one. I can guarantee that when they do come out, I will not be the first one in line to own one. You know, like the people camping out in front of the Apple Store to be the first one to get the latest and greatest new gadget. I will gladly allow these people a place in line for the first personal electronic transporter gadget. Once the atoms or molecules, or whatever the hell that thing does, scatters their particles in places they never dreamed of going and all the bugs get worked out of the device, I'm in. But until the technology is improved to the point of being 100 percent flawless, I guess I'll have to settle for getting felt up by the TSA at my airport gate. Progress? I think not.

But here's the reason I brought up Captain James T. Kirk and the old Star Trek shows. In the shows the starship captain ran his devices. These devices didn't run him. The new technologies have brought many of his devices into reality. Sure, the technology has evolved, yet it's a damn shame the people using them didn't evolve at the same rate. Am I being too harsh here? Certainly not in my observation of the typical smartphone user.

When I get out in the general populace, which by the way is not that frequent, the real disparity hits me. It hits me hardest when I'm traveling by air and happen to be at the airport. Smartphone junkies. Surrounded by them. Running, walking, standing still, sitting, lying across the chairs, running into stuff around them, but all with one glaring similarity. They have an electronic device firmly planted in both hands with their eyes fixed on the screen, that mind-melting cyber stare on their face. To me they kind of look like evil human-sized praying mantises. Something I'm reasonably confident Captain Kirk would blast to hell and back with his phaser.

Now, I realize that at least a few of these evil human-sized praying mantises may actually be doing something productive on their device. But a lot of them? I doubt it. Can't say for sure though. I've never even picked up a smartphone let alone tried to accomplish something useful with it. I also firmly believe that they can choose to live their lives any way they see fit as long as they're not harming someone else. Yet with the sheer number of these evil human-sized praying mantises, I cannot help but be concerned for them. It's not what they're doing on their device but what they're missing by being glued to the damn thing. Life does not happen on a smartphone or a tablet. It happens in your mind, your spirit, and everything that surrounds you.

It cannot happen properly if your mind is always on your device, your spirit has been stolen by your device, and you have absolutely no connection with anything surrounding you except your device. Could be a great horror movie: *The Smartphone That Ate My Brain*. You may feel I'm being a little extreme about the effect smartphones and tablets are having on the general population, but I feel this is something that's been developing for many years. And it's not a positive development. Think I'm kidding?

Douglas Rushkoff, author of the book *Present Shock* puts it this way:

> It's far more difficult, and counterproductive, to attempt to engage into active tasks at once. We cannot write a letter while reconciling the checkbook or, as the rising accident toll indicates,

drive while sending a text message. Yet the more we use the Internet to conduct our work and lives, the more compelled we are to adopt its processors underlying strategy. The more choices are on offer, the more windows remain open, and the more options lie waiting. Each open program is another mouth for our attention to feed.

The competition for our attention is fierce. Back in the mid-1990s, *Wired* magazine announced to the world that although digital real estate was infinite, human attention was finite; there are only so many "eyeball hours" in a day per human. This meant that the new market, the new scarcity, would be over human attention itself. Sticky websites were designed to keep eyeballs glued to particular spots on the Internet, while compelling sounds were composed to draw us to check on incoming message traffic. In a world where attention is the new commodity, it is no surprise the diagnosis of the formerly obscure attention deficit disorder are now so commonplace as to be conferred by school guidance counselors. Since that *Wired* cover in 1997, Ritalin prescriptions have gone up tenfold.

I think I'll make my first billion dollars designing a twelve-step program to disconnect people from their smartphones. I'd be earning my money. And don't think for one minute my twelve-step program idea is far off the mark. In 2013 Bradford Regional Medical Center launched the first hospital-based Internet Addiction Treatment and Recovery Program in the United States. No, I'm not kidding. The program is an intensive ten-day digital treatment and stabilization program under the care of a multidisciplinary medical team. It is directed by Kimberly Young PsyD, who happens to be, get this one, an internationally renowned expert in Internet addiction treatment. Dr. Young had the idea to start the treatment center years ago because she received calls every week asking if she knew of a clinic or hospital that treated Internet addiction. There were none in the United States. Well, thanks, Doc, there are now.

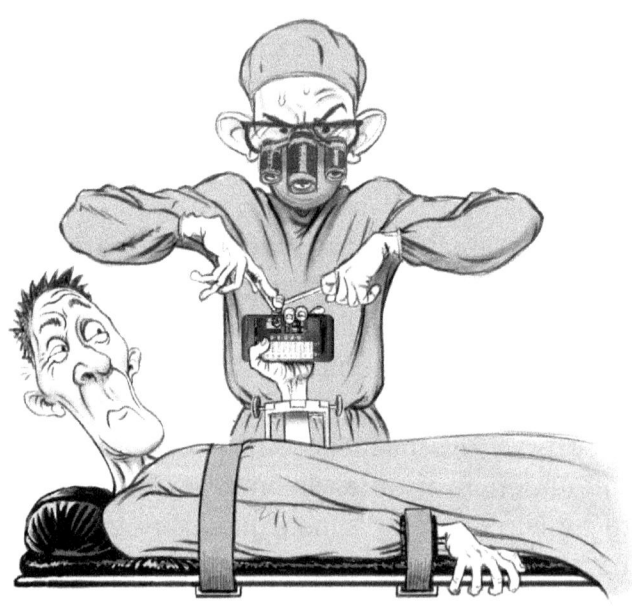

According to Dr. Young, Internet addiction has become an epidemic and public health crisis in countries such as China, Korea, and Taiwan but only recently has Internet addiction been recognized in the United States as a serious problem. In May of 2013, Internet gaming disorder, for the first time, was recognized in the DSM-5, the bible of American psychiatric medicine. They may be a little slow as I recognized it long before they did. Can you imagine walking into the Bradford Regional's program ward with a smartphone in your hand? My guess is it would be like walking into an intensive weight-loss clinic with a hot pizza. I have to give credit to Dr. Young though. She saw the smartphone junkie thing coming back in the mid-1990s. You can even test yourself to see how serious of an addiction problem you may have on her website at Netaddiction.com where she has an Internet Addiction Test you can take online. Kudos to you, Dr. Young.

For the life of me, I cannot understand why all of this 24-7 connectedness appears to be so appealing to so many people. I've never had it explained to me in any way that makes it appear to be anything other than a distracting time suck and cyber waste of one's life. Of course, it's likely you disagree, and if you can help make any legitimate sense of why you choose to be a smartphone zombie, please go to this book's website at Deadguyonfacebook.com and attempt to explain your addiction. But I warn you, if your explanation proves to be just another whiny bastard, *Steve, I like to stay connected to my friends and family with my device* sort of explanation, be prepared for castration or worse. You want to really get your friends and family's attention? Sit down and write them a letter. Although you'd probably want to also do that on your smartphone.

What could possibly be worse than a hard-core smartphone junkie? How about the stupid, idiotic, and painfully pointless apps the digital addict chooses to put on his or her electronic tether. I can't make this shit up. I don't need to. OK, would you like to record your bowel habits to share them with your friends and family? No problem. A couple bucks buys you a program called *Poop The World* where you can keep track of your bowel movements in real time and share them with your friends and family on Facebook. Right down to the size, smell, texture, and even the GPS location where you pinched off the last loaf. Imagine the possibilities? An asshole putting his asshole on Facebook. It would not surprise me if some fecal freak developer came up with a deluxe version of *Poop The World* allowing for automatic uploads of images of your latest great movement and also videos of the flush. Maybe even a little plunger action. This, of course, would likely lead to contested events on Facebook for PTW users and possibly even a Golden Crapper Award. What an aspiration it is to land yourself in the Pooper's Hall of Fame.

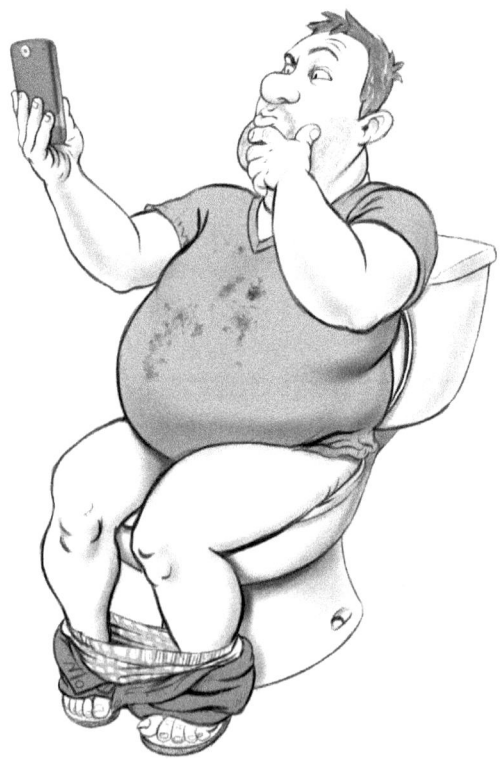

While we're talking body functions here, how about a smartphone app called *Pull My Finger*? This app allows users to pull a virtual finger on their device generating a gleeful sound bite of digital flatulence. But get this. When this app first came out in 2008, it was purchased on Apple's App Store more than fifty thousand times in the first week. *Come on over baby, whole lot of fartin' going on.* Wait, it gets worse. By 2009 there was an actual court battle going on over smartphone fart supremacy in the App Store. In a bold move of digital flatulence domination, *iFart*, another gassy app released around the same time as PMF, sued the company selling PMF over its attempt to trademark the name of its product in the first place. *iFart* claimed it to be a common phrase that could not be protected by trademark and copyright and claimed damages. Obviously proud of their gassy app, in their complaint for declaratory judgment filed in US District Court on February 13, 2009, *iFart* described their product as far superior to that of PMF, explaining that their mobile product simulates twenty different sounds of passing gas, from short toots (the "Butt Socket"), to longer drawn out farts (the "Wipe Out"), to every conceivable way of breaking wind in between. These developers' mothers must be so proud of their children and their digitalized wind biscuits.

Not that I'm dissing the developers for coming up with these applications. I admire and applaud entrepreneurship. I just didn't realize one could make a profit from developing and selling mindless digital methane. Yet it's been my observation that serious smartphone junkies are also seriously gullible consumers when purchasing apps for their digital devices. One such application titled *FatBurner2K* claims to turn your smartphone into the gym that works on your terms. Really? Those terms, one can only assume, are sitting on the couch watching *Pawn Stars* reruns while stuffing one's face with garbage. And *FatBurner's* secret? You lay your smartphone on your rotund midsection, six inches above your belly button, and *FatBurner* causes your device to vibrate. Allegedly miraculously transforming your corpulent carcass from Mr. Jelly Belly to that of Mr. Spectacular Stud Six-Pack Abs. Yeah, right. If we could only get some before and after pictures. On second thought, no thanks.

How about an app that, at least on its surface, appears to be quite useful yet is a stealth technology that could have come right out of the National Security Agency (NSA) playbook? Seriously. A company called Goldenshores Technologies came up with an app called the *Brightest Flashlight Free* app that has been downloaded tens of millions of times. The app turns your smartphone screen into a very bright flashlight. Seems quite handy for repairing that flat tire on a rural road at night or locating that piece of toenail shrapnel that went flying out of the nail cutters onto your bathroom floor. Useful, convenient, and free. Shouldn't Goldenshores receive some sort of humanitarian award for coming up with such a useful application and then choosing to give it away? Ah, no. That's because the developer of this particular application leaves you in the dark about what else the app does besides providing a bright light projecting from your smartphone screen. What it really does would have all the directors of the national security agency high-fiving each other over this one.

The app provides your smartphone with a unique device identifier and tracks your smartphone's precise location 24-7. In other words this developer knows everywhere you go every time you have your smartphone with you and the device is powered up. Not only do they collect this incredible amount of data from their free app, they also turn around and sell this information to numerous third parties. Data brokers, advertising networks, and many other companies that monitor consumer activity. Damn, privacy may not be dead yet, but it sure as hell is on life support.

Another app competing in the spectacularly stupid smartphone application competition is one simply called *Kiss Me*. This application allegedly evaluates the user's ability to kiss. Smartphone junkies are invited to kiss the phone, well, actually its touch screen, and after the smooch the program will rate this kiss on a ten-point scale. It tells users about how much time and attention they put into the kiss. In this app's description, the developer claims, "You'll be the life of the party sharing this hilarious kissing game with friends! Pull out your best lip locking skills and challenge this app." OK, I may not be smartphone savvy, but it would seem to me, at least, that a more accurate evaluation of one's kissing abilities should be provided by another human being. Could smartphone junkies with the *Kiss Me* app actually be this passionate about their device? Apparently so. Go ahead; pucker up to your touch screen. No tongue though.

There are, of course, smartphone applications designed for one purpose that are used more often for totally different purposes. One such app is the astoundingly popular *Snapchat* photo-sharing app that allows you to quickly send images or videos to your friends that will then disappear from their smartphones in seconds. I suppose handy for sending a brief image of a garage sale find to the local antique dealer or sending granny a quick picture so she can see her grandchildren playing at the park. I can even think of instances where I would use this app, like when my wife asked me to pick up a half gallon of milk while I was at the grocery store, and to my surprise I discovered they currently stock forty-seven different kinds of milk. Who knew? But apparently the biggest reason for the popularity of the *Snapchat* app is to send naughty pictures to friends or lovers without having to worry about the recipient keeping the pictures of your privates and plastering them all over the web. A good thing I'd say. After all, if you can't keep it in your boxers, your panties, or your bra, at least keep it off of the web. Dirty pictures have been around since the times of the caveman, but thanks to the *Snapchat* app you will not be immortalizing yourself with them. I would guess that Anthony Weiner likely has this app on his smartphone. Heck, if he had stuck to *Snapchat* with his wiener pictures, he'd probably still be a congressman. As unfortunate but true as that is.

Photos aren't unique to the self-destruction applications as there are also apps available to self-destruct your text messages, e-mails, call lists, and even porn-site visits. Nearly anything you would want to keep masked from prying eyes on your smartphone. Seems the biggest users of these applications are people who are cheating on their spouse or their lover. Funny thing is, according to a survey conducted by the affairs and dating site Victoria Milan, 45 percent of smartphone users have either cheated or at least contemplated cheating on their partner because the other person pays too much attention to their smartphone. Gotta love the irony of that. One such application simply called *CATE*, which stands for call and text eraser, evaporates those pesky call lists to your paramour and those flirtatious text messages to your latest affair. Another slick application called *Vaulty Stocks* looks like an app for checking the stock market, but actually it is a hidden treasure chest on your device that hides all of your naughty pictures and videos from anyone curiously checking out your smartphone.

There is a flipside of the coin to these cheating apps. One such application that I found particularly amusing, maybe even a bit unsettling, is the app called *Flexispy. Flexispy* allows you to get all the dirt in real time on what your partner's up to on their smartphone. You can listen in on their calls, track their location, view their text messages, read their e-mails, and even place a bug on them by turning their device into a microphone. No, I'm not making this up. I don't need to. Higher-priced versions of this application will even allow you to turn your suspected lover's device into a video camera. *I'll be snooping on my sweetie this Friday night. Film at eleven.* Are you kidding me? So how does the developer get away with this extreme violation of privacy? Pretty much the same way the NSA does; they lie a lot to spin it in a positive direction. The following is taken right from their website at flexispy.com:

> We understand that our products literally change lives, not a responsibility we take lightly, and we know how important your privacy is, so we do everything possible to ensure that your spouse does not discover the software. Flexispy invented the spy phone in 2005, and we continue to design, develop, test and support all of our own products in the house, under one unified team, nothing is outsourced, so you get a decade worth of technology craftsmanship that has been tested by over a million customers. Finally, we provide a genuine ten-day money back guarantee, with no fine print, and the support team that really know the products, so you don't get frustrated by people reading from scripts.

Of course, as we have experienced with the NSA here in the United States, this type of sneaky spying doesn't come cheap. The application starts at $149 per year and goes all the way up to $349 per year for the extreme edition. I suppose that maybe your pit bull lawyer could recover your investment in the divorce decree.

There are, of course, reasons for the growing multitude of smartphone apps that assist you in hooking up with your illicit lover or masking your smartphone contents from your lover or spouse. The biggest reason being a condition that has been coined infomania. And what is infomania? Nothing more than a politically correct term to call someone who is a smartphone junkie. Yet, any marriage counselor worth his or her salt, would be the first to tell you that infomania is ruining more relationships than free hookers. Seriously. You are probably nodding your head in agreement if you happen to have a current spouse or lover who is an infomaniac, a smartphone junkie. Do you prefer to spend your evenings on your device exchanging messages rather than speaking to your husband? Do you keep your smartphone by your bed and even use it while in the bathroom or eating dinner? Are you so distracted by your device at bedtime that sex is off the agenda? Well, if you are in a serious relationship and you also happen to be a smartphone junkie, or excuse me, an infomaniac, then I can pretty much guarantee you that your relationship is or will soon be in serious trouble. After all, there is simply no way you can pay that much attention to your device while paying adequate attention to your partner. And if you do not pay adequate attention to your partner, he or she will eventually start looking elsewhere. Who knows, if your partner is also an infomaniac, his or her device may be the elsewhere your partner looks. My only question is, who's going to get the *Flexispy* app first?

As a kid I was raised in a Catholic household. As a family we went to a Catholic church every Sunday, and my siblings and I were also required at a young age to attend a catechism class at the church one night a week because we went to a public grade school. While I commend my parents in their attempt to expose me at a young age to religion, spirituality, and oneness with God, I will admit that I have not been a practicing Catholic since my late teens. My reasons for this are unimportant. I just wanted to share with you that I still have a basic understanding of the Catholic faith. Because of this understanding, I can pretty much guarantee you that somewhere in a classroom at this very moment, there is a really pissed off nun wielding a wooden yardstick, crushing the knuckles of one of her catechism students for not obeying the rules and putting away his or her digital smartphone tether during her class. It's a nun's modus operandi—that Catholic guilt thing plus intense pain. And most likely, in this day and age, the bloody-knuckled smartphone-junkie kid would whimper in reply, *But, Sister, I was on a Catholic website. Shouldn't that count for some extra credit here?* Whack, for a second time.

In the Catholic faith, there is a sacrament simply entitled "confession." This is a simple, albeit awkward, process of sitting in a broom-closet-sized room adjoining another broom closet occupied by a priest. There is a dense screen in between so you can hear each other, yet identification and eye contact is all but impossible. Catholics are asked to occupy the confessional and recount their sins to a priest confessor, who in turn doles out penance, usually in the form of prayers. This sacrament is the Catholic way of coming clean and repenting for all of your wrongdoings since the last time you occupied the holy broom closet, and the penance issued and carried out is said to cleanse your soul, at least to the point where your spirit is again clean enough to accept the Holy Spirit in your life.

This was a very uncomfortable process as a child, and the dread I felt before and after my trip to the holy broom closet was probably a sin in and of itself. As I grew older, I better understood the process of repenting my misdeeds and asking the Lord's forgiveness, but to this day I've never understood why the Catholic faith would require a middleman, of sorts, to do so. I mean really, if I wish to speak with my maker about some rather personal issues in my life, is it really required that I go through one of his earthly agents?

Things have changed in the years since then thanks to technology and our digital devices. It appears that some confessors, Catholic priests charged with the task of cleansing one's soul from the broom closet, would like to introduce an easier way for the flock to seek out this sanitization. This easier way is the imminent arrival of a new smartphone app called *My Confessor*. According to the *New York Daily News* the *My Confessor* app will allow the faithful to keep up digitally with when their local priest is hearing confession. When accessed, the app will reportedly portray a red status box that means "Father is OUT" or a green status box that means "Father is IN." It also includes a description of reconciliation as well as related tips. According to the app's website at myconfessor.org, this application allows you to see if there is a priest available for confessions in your area. It also offers a tutorial on the proper manners of making confession. Finally, the app offers an examination of conscience so when you prepare to spill your guts in the holy broom closet, there's no concern over missing a few black marks lurking in your soul. Will a digital device and application wind up replacing the trip to the holy broom closet anytime in the near future? Only time will tell, but until then I can only think of one question I would like answered about this app: *does the Pope know about this?*

There are many apps for smartphone junkies to automate their connection between their devices and social media sites. How about an app to disconnect them? Three cheers for Scott Garner who calls himself a "basically unemployable" designer and developer. Garner built the app called *Hell is Other People*. On his website he calls it an experiment in "antisocial media." On the site he notes, "This project is partially a satire, partially a commentary on my disdain for social media, and partially an exploration of my own difficulties with social anxiety." The app utilizes you and your friends' Foursquare accounts, tracking the check-ins and calculating a map of the optimal locations for you to go to actually avoid them. Pretty nifty if you happen to be running late, are not in the mood for any type of human interaction, or were unsuccessful at effectively masking that huge zit that grew on your forehead overnight. Though I suppose if you were truly serious about exhibiting a measure of antisocial behavior, the first choice would be to shut off your smartphone and put the damn thing away. How antisocial!

There are some smartphone apps out there that, at least through my eyes, just plain shouldn't be in existence. One that quickly comes to mind is an app called *Name Tag*. *Name Tag* puts the "creep" in creepy and the "stalk" in stalker. Sit back and imagine for a moment that you are a young lady on a Saturday morning at the farmers market picking up some fresh local foods to make Sunday dinner for you and your children. While waiting in line at the Italian booth for your number to be called, you are approached by a creepy looking guy with a bad comb-over and a smartphone in his hand. He says that after you are finished with your purchase, he would be happy to buy you a kiwi margarita because he knows that is your favorite drink. Damn, he's right. How lucky of a guess could that be? You nervously tell him that's not possible because you need to get home to your children. He tells you your son and daughters are just fine and are eating breakfast at the next-door neighbor's house. How in the world did he know that? *Name Tag*.

Mr. Creepy then tries to continue a conversation with you, and it is simply uncanny the things he states that he has in common with you. He knows you have three children, that you are divorced, and that you love to water ski at the lake in the summer. He also knows where you work and where you graduated from college. Suddenly, you come to realize that all of the information he's providing about you could be located on your social media pages and also on that dating website you signed up for last month, hoping to finally meet the right guy. You are correct, but Mr. Creepy did this almost instantly with his *Name Tag* app on his smartphone. Turns out Mr. Creepy surreptitiously took a picture of you waiting in line at the Italian booth from his smartphone and uploaded the picture to a server where it was then compared to millions of head shots on the Internet. Thanks to the powerful facial recognition software, Mr. Creepy now has all of your social media profiles and dating profile on the device in his sweaty little palm. Who on earth would ever think this technology-heavy app is really a good idea? The developers.

The landing page of the *Name Tag* website at nametag.ws sells their disturbing belief in this app:

> With *Name Tag*, your photo shares you. Why leave amazing people up to chance? Don't miss out on the opportunity to connect with others who share your passions! Connect your info and interests with the world by simply sharing your most unique feature—your face. *Name Tag* links your face to a single unified online presence that includes your contact information, your social media profiles, interests, hobbies and passions and anything else you want to share with the world. Using the *Name Tag* smartphone or Google Glass app, simply snap a picture of someone you want to connect with and see their entire public online presence in one place. Don't be a stranger.

Don't be a stranger? Are you kidding me? How about don't be an invasive asshole by trying to impress a young girl by taking a picture of her and pushing a button on your asshole smartphone app? I swear to God, if anyone ever pulls this *Name Tag* app crap on me, I'm going to permanently name tag their face beyond any kind of recognition.

One of my biggest concerns, being an individual who generally shuns mobile devices, living in a world of evil human-sized praying mantises, is that, at least in my observation, I am rapidly becoming a minority. Never underestimate the power of smartphone junkies to breed and multiply. Although I am surprised they can peel themselves away from their devices long enough to do so. OK, maybe there's an app for that too. I suppose my only real concern is that all of this connectedness causes a complete disconnect from the real world in many of these digital victims. You've seen it, I've seen it, and likely everyone has seen it: an evil human-sized praying mantis walking into a street light pole, running into you physically in an airport terminal, posting fireworks pictures on their Facebook page versus sitting back and enjoying the show, maybe even stepping in front of a moving bus. Splat, game over. But the smartphone is still humming anyway.

Not only are they disconnected from the world around them because of their digital addiction but they are increasingly disconnecting from their spouses and their children. According to CBS News, in a recent study, researchers from Boston University Medical Center camped out in Boston area fast-food places between July and August 2013. The researchers stated in a report that they hope their findings will help generate additional research and discussion about the use of smartphone technology around children. Their findings raise questions about the long-term effects on child development when parents and caregivers, like nannies, are frequently absorbed with their digital devices when spending time with the kids. Researchers observed fifty-five interactions with caregivers and young children and wrote detailed notes on what they saw, describing all aspects of any mobile device use and how kids and caregivers reacted during these times. At no time were the researchers approached by others in the restaurant about their surveillance.

They spotted forty caregivers using their smartphones during their meal; only fifteen did not. The most absorbed parents were swiping something with their fingers, perhaps surfing the web, reading or playing a game, compared to the least absorbed parents who just took phone calls. All of their attention was firmly on their device, and they rarely put it down to talk with other people within the group. They seemed to be more engaged in the device than with the children they cared for. Of these forty interactions, the children exhibited behavior that ranged from entertaining themselves to escalating bids to get their caregiver's attention, such as by being silly and acting out. The more absorbed the caregivers were in their devices, the more likely they were to respond harshly to their child's bad behavior. For example, one female caregiver staring at her smartphone with a baby in her lap yelled at her two other boys: "Just two more minutes, please eat." One of the boys lost his straw in his juice box, and the same caregiver looked up from her phone and said he couldn't have it anymore since he pushed it in.

In another observation a child got up to walk across the restaurant to get ketchup and the caregiver didn't even look up. At one point she stared into her phone for about two minutes without ever looking away, and she had no conversation with the kids throughout most of the meal.

In another observation a girl would play with her food and start stabbing a container with her fork until she was scolded by both parents, both looking at their phones throughout. The researchers said these provocative behaviors may have been expressed to test limits. Other episodes did not involve harsh reactions from caregivers, including a woman who would nod without looking up while her girl asked her questions, with a child continuing to sway in her chair and ask away. The more absorbed caregivers kept their gaze on the device while answering questions or giving instructions, often in a scolding or robotic tone, if they even responded to the attention-seeking behavior in the kids at all. The researchers cautioned this study was a first step in looking into whether mobile devices are particularly more absorbing than other activities that parents often have to multitask when caring for a child, and conclusions about how smartphones affect child-parent interaction should not be drawn.

You don't need to be a researcher at Boston University Medical Center to realize that the findings in the study are watered down to plain vanilla. How about a little Tabasco sauce? Even though I am encouraged that there are such studies as these being carried out, I often wonder why the researchers don't just plain call people out on it. After all, if you are in care of your children or someone else's kids, shouldn't you be paying at least some attention to them? And how in the world are these little kids ever going to learn to carry an adult conversation when every time they are sitting at a table with adults, the kids are completely shunned because the adults are too absorbed in whatever they're doing on their smartphone.

I witnessed a perfect example of this recently while I was traveling. First, when I do travel, I nearly always stay in a first-class hotel. Just my thing I suppose. On this particular trip, my wife and I and some friends were staying the night in Terre Haute, Indiana, near where my daughter goes to college. I'm not sure what type of people would have the occasion to stay at a hotel in Terre Haute, but I'm dead certain that it's not people like me.

Why do I say this? Because in Terre Haute, Indiana, there are no first-class hotels. None. Understand that my idea of roughing it isn't something like going camping or RVing or taking a canoe trip down the river. My idea of roughing it is staying in a hotel that does not have a cocktail lounge or a concierge. Well, I got rooms in Terre Haute for my wife and me, and our friends, to attend our daughter's college event. I found it odd that the place was called Comfort Suites. Because what it was lacking in comfort certainly wasn't being made up by what they had in suites. That's because there were none. Our room was the size of my bathroom, and smaller than the size of the bathroom in my suite at Caesars Palace.

Anyway, after we checked into our rooms, I poured myself a bourbon on the rocks and went in pursuit of a quiet place to enjoy the beverage and a cigar. I wound up outside the entrance of the indoor pool, sitting in a smoke hole at a crappy picnic table. But my eyes were really opened after I finished my vices when I cut through the swimming pool area to get back to my room. There were about fifteen kids running around and splashing in the pool with seven adults sitting in the lounge chairs. Of course, the adults were there to monitor the children and make sure little Johnny wasn't attempting to drown his little sister. Yet little Johnny could have whacked her with no problem when you looked at these adults. All seven of them had 100 percent of their attention buried in the bright screens of their devices. I don't know, maybe it's just me who gets bugged by crap like this, or maybe these seven had some sort of lifeguard app on their devices.

Reminds me of another situation I witnessed recently when my wife and I went to a ballroom for a dance. Halfway through the dance, we decided to sit on the sidelines for a song or two to rest our legs and have a beverage. We joined two other dancers, who were also taking a break, at their table. While my wife and I were admiring the moves of the other dancers on the floor, what were the two dancers sitting at our table doing? That's right, staring into their smartphone screens and swiping them feverishly with a free finger. In a ballroom, during the dance, with their attention totally consumed by their devices. I do not understand, and, furthermore, I do not want to understand. I refuse to become part of the digitally tethered majority. If you showed up tonight to do the foxtrot, try doing it on the dance floor, instead of on the touch screen of your digital device.

But should the untethered growing minority be concerned? Certainly not for ourselves. Being connected to our real world and our real lives instead of our devices places us firmly in a far more favorable position than the praying mantis types. Where our concerns should really go is to the future generations of smartphone zombies. I mean, I'm no conspiracy theorist here, but what if this was some sort of sick government plot to dumb down our future generations into mind-controlled, screen-gazing, drooling zombies? If that were truly the case, I would say the plot is working beyond their wildest dreams. Yet is there really a way that could effectively save these future generations from having their brains turned to instant pudding by their smartphones? I don't have one, but I know someone who does.

Best-selling author, and my favorite business coach, Dan S. Kennedy came up with a plan to save people from being smartphone junkies and also solve the national debt crisis in the United States at the very same time. Kind of a two for one. Dan's plan is that the federal government should begin issuing hunting licenses at the rate of maybe $10,000 a pop. And what will these hunters be hunting? You guessed it—evil human-sized praying mantis types. That would get their attention. These special hunting licenses would be issued with only three requirements. First, you've got the extra dough to spend. Second, only one kill allowed per license. And third, you must aim for the smartphone. Brilliant.

OK, maybe a bit extreme for your taste, but let me ask you a question. Wouldn't it be a better world if occasionally a lot of stupidity came with a little pain and suffering? I mean, at least then people might devote a sliver of thought and contemplation to not making idiots of themselves. Don't get me wrong here. I'm not condoning violence. I never condone violence, but I certainly understand it. Not the violent type? That's OK—it's your choice. But tell me about your plan to save these people from their devices. Any ideas? I didn't think so.

I do not believe I've ever heard anyone state that as a prerequisite to using a smartphone, the user needs to be smart. As a matter of fact, much compelling evidence exists to the contrary. Take, for instance, a tragic story from the *Chicago Tribune*. Roger Mirro, fifty-six, told a neighbor in his apartment complex in suburban Chicago that he may have dropped his smartphone down the garbage chute in his apartment. Mirro asked for the key to the trash room in the lower-level parking garage. Around three and a half hours later, police got a call from Mirro's wife stating he was missing. After talking to neighbors, officers searched the parking garage and the trash room where they discovered a lock had been removed from the door. They saw a ladder propped up alongside the trash compactor and found Mirro's body inside it. Evidently, the gent did a little Dumpster diving for his smartphone, not realizing the Dumpster was actually a compactor, and when it cycled, Mirro became one with his smartphone. I can only hope Mirro's life insurance policy covered tragic stupidity as a cause of death.

What do you get when you cross a not-too-bright smartphone user with a really dim-witted burglar? According to the *Fayetteville Observer*, you get a young North Carolina man by the name of Anthony Dubeos Graham. Mr. Graham burglarized a home in Spring Lake, North Carolina, stealing a smartphone in the process. What does the young thief do with the stolen swag? No, he doesn't try to fence the thing for a little extra pocket cash; he decides to play with the device. He takes pictures of himself with the stolen gadget, flashing gang signs, smoking cigarettes, and looking like the young punk he is. He then uploads the pictures to the victim's Facebook account. Brilliant Anthony. At least, after seeing the images of himself on the evening news, he came to his senses enough to turn himself in, according to the Cumberland County Sheriff's Office. One count each of breaking and entering, larceny, and possessing stolen property, and you might as well throw in one count of criminal idiocy. Can you imagine what his cell mates will say? How can the judge even keep a straight face?

Apparently, Mr. Graham doesn't have a lock on doing really stupid things with stolen smartphones. As I was writing this book, a story broke about a German woman named Laura Falafel who was on the beach with friends in Ibiza when her smartphone got stolen. In an interview with *Metro News*, Laura tells her story.

Q: What happened in Ibiza?
Laura: Me and my friends were enjoying a night skinny dipping in the sea, but when I returned to the beach, I noticed my smartphone was gone as well as my passport and money. We wanted to call the police immediately, but the receptionist at our hotel said we'd have to wait until the morning as they won't come for theft crimes. I felt really helpless and alone there and then.

Q: When did you discover the photos?
Laura: Back in Germany, four months after the Ibiza trip. It was a few days after Christmas. I turned on my computer and noticed fifteen new pictures inside my Dropbox upload folder. At first, I didn't know what was going on. But then the penny dropped. One month before that, a guy used my Skype account and called all of my female friends to hit on them. At first I thought this was some kind of Skype error or misunderstanding. But then I figured out that it must have been the guy, I now call him "Hafid," who has my phone as it had my Skype details there.

Q: Did you want to get your phone back?
Laura: No, actually. I have found peace with the situation. And when I saw the pictures, I got inspired and got the idea for a blog because Hafid lives in

Dubai, and life there is really interesting. There are photos of him beside the world's tallest building and with friends in front of a mosque and posing next to cool cars. This is much better than any smartphone in the world.

Q: Have you been in touch with the police?
Laura: Yes, first I went to them in Ibiza, and then after I got the pictures as evidence, I went to the German police too. But it took them about six months to tell me that they had stopped the investigation.

Q: Did you expect that your blog would be so popular?
Laura: Not at all! Who would expect something like that? It's been incredible though. This is the awesome thing about the Internet when things go viral. In just one week my blog got two million hits and seventeen thousand followers.

The thing I can't figure out about this story is who is the stupidest. Hafid? Maybe Laura? Perhaps the seventeen thousand followers watching the smartphone thief's every move? I don't know, and I could use your help. If you'd like to help me in figuring it out, you can find Laura's blog here: lifeofastrangerwhostolemyphone.tumblr.com

So what are your options if someone who steals your smartphone is not quite as foolish as Anthony or Hafid? With the ever-expanding black market for these stolen devices, it's something you should consider, especially if you are a smartphone junkie. How about having your device replicate what Anthony or Hafid did? You can—there's an app for it. Mobile security-software maker Lookout announced an app called *Lock Cam* that might help you recover that stolen smartphone or tablet. Once someone tries and fails three times to unlock your password-protected gadget, the app will stealthily take and e-mail you a photo of that person and their location. In my eyes this is not effective for the savvy professional thief, but who said you had to be smart to be a crook? Besides, I'm skeptical about this app catching many bad guys. It's more likely that users will start getting e-mails containing photos of their pets, or even worse, a photo of themselves drunk last night trying to call a cab. *What in the hell was that password again?*

After my kid proudly received her first smartphone, it didn't take me long to realize that nearly anyone can design and manufacture cheap plastic crap, and if this crap is marketed as a smartphone accessory, it will sell and sell well. I have to hand it to these manufacturers and designers because they have essentially turned these electronic tethers into fashion statements. Oh, my dear, those beautiful shoes match your handbag perfectly, but I feel compelled to mention that you really need to do something about your smartphone. It is so not you. I did not realize just how prolific this cheap plastic crap was until I was writing this section of the book. I went to Amazon.com and looked up cell phone accessories, finding that they had 5.8 million smartphone cases available, 62,000 holsters and clips, 15,000 armbands, and 129,000 screen protectors. Through anyone's eyes that's a lot of cheap plastic crap.

The total number of cell phone accessories available on the website is just north of 8.5 million items. They are, however, not all cheap plastic crap. If you would like your device to be charming, there are over 102,000 smartphone charms available on Amazon, including a cute little panda bear charm that will set you back $10,000. Or you might be interested in a three-piece stylus pen set for your touchscreen, three different fashionable colors, of course, that will set you back an even grand. Shipping included. A company called DIMA is marketing a titanium case for the iPhone 5 that is embellished with 576 real diamonds. At $12,000 plus $10 shipping, it's likely you will be the only one of your friends to own one. The iPhone 5 is included in the price, but if you're interested you'd better hurry. The site currently has only one left in stock. Or if you're on a budget, you can score a Nokia Arte Gold 24 karat classic gold luxury mobile phone for $3000.

Apparently, the smartphone fashion industry is not limiting itself to doodads and dress-ups for your device alone. The high-tech apparel industry appears to have taken notice to the growing amount of smartphone junkies in the world and is now producing slacks, jeans, jackets, and shirts designed to fit your device so you can view it without even taking it out of its special pocket. Much of this apparel promises that you can now rest at ease because you no longer need to suffer through that "smartphone bulge." One such company, I/O Denim, has even produced a comical groin-grabbing ad to accompany their latest garb. You can watch their silly slice of human stupidity by simply going to YouTube and searching the words "Too Tight for a Cell Phone." Both comedy and tragedy in this little thirty second spot. Comedy because it's really funny to watch, yet tragedy because it is frighteningly accurate.

Children becoming smartphone junkies at an early age are proving to be a concern, at least to some. In fact, in Kariya City, Japan, around thirteen thousand schoolchildren between the ages of six and fifteen have been banned from using mobile technology in the evenings. The technology curfew move reportedly aims to discourage children from spending an unhealthy amount of time on electronic devices such as smartphones. The ban, which was initially proposed by a group of teachers, social workers and police, was not officially issued by city hall, so parents will not face any penalty if their children do not comply, according to Japanese media reports. However, the initiative is reportedly supported by Kariya's Board of Education as well as all twenty-one schools across the city, with parents being directly requested to remove smartphones after nine o'clock and monitor the websites their children access.

As a parent I believe my biggest concern about the growing number of smartphone junkies is when I see little kids walking down the street in their evil little-human-sized praying mantis pose, smartphone clamped in their mitts, and eyeballs plastered to the screen. Something in my gut tells me that when these little kids reach adulthood, they will wind up with the attention span and communication skills of a fruit fly. I could be wrong, and I hope that I am. After all, when I was their age, many adults thought that because of rock 'n' roll, my generation would grow up sterile, and our ears would fall off. Hasn't happened yet, and, unbelievably, the Rolling Stones are still touring. Yet this still doesn't mean that my concerns are not well-founded. Just the thought of these little kids in adult bodies becoming fear stricken and dysfunctional when detached from their devices is just plain sickening to me. No, it's not a sign of the times. It's a sign of addiction.

Of course, the addiction also has a name. Nomophobia. The term is an abbreviation for no-mobile-phone phobia, and according to a study done in the United Kingdom, it creates high anxiety in over half of mobile phone users when they misplace their smartphone, run out of battery power, or are located temporarily where there is no network coverage. Numerous technology companies have come up with innovative products for nomophobics to help alleviate their anxiety when they run out of battery in their smartphones. Especially if they run out of battery where there is no electricity available. There is a hand turbine smartphone charger that will charge your device by simply turning a crank. No surprise to me, in this charger's description there's no mention of cranking time versus charging time. Guess you could sit around the campfire with this charger and have the kids crank.

Another cranking option is a bike-charge dynamo that hooks up to the wheel of your bicycle and will charge your smartphone as you pedal merrily along. Make sure to keep your eyes on the road instead of on your device, or you'll likely find yourself somewhere in the hedges, or worse. There are numerous alternative charging devices that operate off of heat, be it a camp stove, a teapot, or even a coffee cup. Solar options are also numerous whether in the form of a window-stuck solar panel, a solar-panel sunflower charger, and even solar-panel-lined backpacks. What's a nomophobe to do on cloudy days or after dark? Simple. There are wind-powered chargers you can use to bring that smartphone battery back to life. Strap it to your arm and go jogging. Strap it to the handlebars on your bicycle and take a ride. Strap it to the window of the bus during your commute home from work. And if your smartphone doesn't charge quickly enough, you can always strap it to your ass and go jump off a bridge. Take a deep breath and turn the page because we will be discussing social media junkies next.

Social Media Junkies

And you thought I was just going to pick on Facebook in this book? Wrong, dead wrong. The social media scene is getting sillier by the minute, and I could not help but take a jab at some of this digital silliness. You are, or at least you should be, responsible and fully in charge of all of your online content. Especially content placed on social media sites. Your digital diary will live on through the sites long after the check for your life insurance policy has been cashed. Yet if you look at the majority of online content placed on the Internet by the typical social media junkie, it does not leave a favorable impression of the time you spent here among the living. But what if you could somehow make amends for all of your social media psychobabble by leaving one last favorable message on all of your social media pages after you do check out of this lifetime? You can—seriously.

With app services available like *ifidie.net*, you can prerecord a video, prewrite your final social media post, or even compose that final text message you send out, and the application will publish these for you while the ink is still wet on your death certificate. Kind of like the final paragraph in your online social life. Who knows, it may even be possible for you to acquire more friends, followers, and likes on your social media pages after you have entered the digital afterlife. Although I'm not entirely sure what that would say about how you chose to live your life while you were still among us. So let's take a look at several popular social media sites and apply them to social media junkies.

Facebook is of course number one with over 1.1 billion active users on the site as of this writing. They are actually running out of people in the developed world to become new users on their website. This could be the reason why this particular social media site chooses to lock up in my browser all the time and crawls slowly when it is functioning. Understand I'm a lost puppy in this environment. I rarely visit this site, although, as I explained earlier, my Webmaster set things up where some of my material will go right to my Facebook page through automation. Thank God for that because it appears, at least to me, that on the rare occasion I do happen to go to the website, I can't recognize a damn thing. Everything's changed. And from what I can see, not for the better.

Almost immediately, paid advertising begins sneaking onto the folds, trying to get my attention. How the hell do you make this stuff go away? Then, in an annoyingly magical way, the website itself starts asking me questions. Facebook asks me what city I live in. None of your business. If you're that smart of a website, you'd look my address up all by yourself. Then it wants me to tell it where I went to college. I'm tempted to fill in *Whatsa Matta U*, but I don't believe the Facebook website has much of a penchant for humor. Then it asks me if my wife and kid are on Facebook and what their names are. Thanks but no thanks. I prefer to keep my personal life just that. Personal. At least these are requests that I understand, yet why does it continue to ask me when I refuse to answer?

Then this stupid little message pops up right in front of my photo on the screen: "We've made some updates to how your timeline looks. Your posts and life events are on the right, with everything else on the left." Timeline? Life events? Everything else? What in the hell are they talking about? Maybe it's a good thing; I don't know. If my brain was organized like this damn website, I'd never get a lick of work in during my day. So I have to ask myself, *How in the world did Facebook become the number one social media site on the Internet?* I mean supposedly there are over one billion active users on the site. What's the draw here? Am I missing something? Yeah, probably a lot. And I'm grateful.

I suppose there is an art to how Facebook users build, maintain, and edit their personal pages. Most likely, it's the art of deception. Yet I firmly believe that even an honest and sober attempt to represent yourself on a Facebook page as you are in real life is pretty much an impossibility. Think about it. People are complex, and real life is compound and multifaceted. Facebook pages are not. Yet Facebook requires you to sum up your digital persona into neatly organized categories with brief snippets of both your off-line and online personalities. This makes your online presence highly incongruent with who you really are, or at least should be, in the world outside of the Internet.

Besides, do the things on my Facebook page, like who has friended me, places I've been, information about my work and education, family members, hobbies, sports interests, music appreciation, groups I belong to, and events I've attended, truly define me as a person in real life? Of course not—not even close. In real life these things do not portray you. In real life you should characterize them. Seriously, who in the hell would ever care about the fact that I still love to get down and boogie to the big-band sound of Louis Jordan? Or maybe dial in a little vintage George Clinton from time to time? Or even crank up the song that forty years ago got me thrown out of the high school jazz band. By the way, that would be James Brown's original version of "Sex Machine." I can still recall the bass line that was my demise as a professional musician. Was I just misbehaving and being rebellious, or was it a total lack of appreciation for Brown's arrangements on the part of my high school band teacher? Probably both. But does any of that matter now? Hell no, and it shouldn't. It may have been a moment in my life, but it wasn't a defining moment.

To solidify my point of view on the deceptivity of Facebook pages for this book, I went, for the very first time by the way, to the Facebook page of my wife. Let me start out by saying that she is a loving, caring, and wonderful woman, sensitive to nature in a spiritual way, with a heart of gold that captures the essence of her being. Well, it's a damned good thing I knew all of this about her before my visit to her Facebook page. The first thing that jumped out at me was the picture she chose for her profile, her beautiful smile and sparkling blue eyes, cheek to cheek with a man. By the way, I'm not present in her profile picture. Her chosen profile picture is one of her schmoozing, very closely schmoozing, with celebrity chef author and television star Anthony Bourdain. Luckily, I do not feel in any way threatened by this because I'm the one who actually snapped the photo. Eat your heart out, Tony. She's still mine.

The second thing that got my attention was listed under her basic information. Specifically in the area of items she is interested in. Because she took the time to mention only one thing of interest on her Facebook page. Men. That's it, nothing more. Fortunately, I'm confident this one subject does not represent my wife in real life. In fact, she cares more about her hummingbirds than the majority of men on the planet. I then scrolled down to the photo section of her page. The vast majority of images in this area are of her hugging men. Auspiciously, a few of these photos are even with me. It appears that my wife's online presence can still keep me secure in my manhood and marriage.

It's obvious by her Facebook page that my wife is not a social media junkie. I determine this by the fact that as of this writing, she has 162 friends on the website. My daughter, on the other hand, is sporting 1,304 of them. But what I find interesting about these friends of my wife on Facebook is a little statistic off to the right stating that my wife and I share 35 mutual friends and there are another 25 of her friends that I *may* know. Really? Is this social media site telling me that my loving wife has 102 online friends that her husband wouldn't stand a chance in hell of knowing? That's curious, seeing that outside of the working environment, we spend nearly 100 percent of our free time together. Well, how much time do these 102 mystery online friends spend with her? In person, I would say near zero. And online, not very damn much. Good for her.

There was, however, one thing I discovered on my wife's Facebook page that I can't help but feel is cause for alarm. There are twenty-three people, places, and things listed on her page under the category of other likes. One of these caused me more than a bit of distress. Which of her likes do I find disturbing? Mitt Romney. Unbelievable. Are you kidding me? Looks like I had better devote thirty minutes or so to explaining the real Mitt Romney to my sweetie so she can undo this grave error in judgment. And it should be relatively simple to do so. After all, my wife is originally from Detroit. I'm sure she will quickly be able to get an accurate grasp of what's really going on in the Romney household.

In this little experiment, it quickly became obvious to me that my wife's online persona in no way reflects the wonderful human being she is in real life and in person. Thank God. If it was a true snapshot of the woman I fell in love with and married, I might have to go through digital divorce. Was she trying to deceive anyone when composing her Facebook page? Absolutely not. I know her better than that. I also know that originally she had a kid in the neighborhood set the whole thing up for her. But could you get to know her real personality even a little bit by reviewing her Facebook page? Not a chance.

Curious about this experiment, I went to the Facebook page of a good friend of mine, my brilliant massage therapist, who I also happen to know is a social media junkie. I wanted to see what a true addict does on their Facebook page versus the nonaddicted minority. To my surprise he's not quite as much of a junkie as my daughter because he is only sporting 1,043 friends. On his page it appears we have five mutual friends. One being my wife, another who's a very good friend of mine, two who I know casually, and one guy that I have no idea who the hell he is. OK, I get it. I consider this man a dear friend, but we do not socialize together. And by the looks of his Facebook page, I believe I've figured out why. He wouldn't have the time to socialize with my wife and me. Why? He'd be too busy posting various things to his Facebook timeline. Seriously, I'm looking at his Facebook page on a Friday morning, and there are seventeen different posts on his timeline that were placed there today. Yet I know this man is smart, talented, compassionate, and a highly spiritual individual. Thank God he is professional enough to execute his massage skills with both hands when I'm on his table, his digital devices not even within his reach. God bless him. He may be a social media junkie, but he's still the consummate pro.

To my surprise his Facebook page does not contain the detail I thought I was going to discover. Probably a good thing because he is a highly complex man. It appears he stuck to the basics in the about section of his page with just simple things about his family, his work, his education, and his interests. With all of the publicness on his timeline, I'm refreshed to realize he still cherishes some privacy. It's not the least bit surprising to me that his Facebook page contains 481 photos. Besides being a truly gifted massage therapist, he is also a wildly artistic professional photographer. I'm also quite relieved to discover that my friend is utilizing his personal Facebook page as a means of directing traffic to a page for his massage business and also to his photography website. Got to pay the bills. Might as well have your 1,043 Facebook friends help you out in that department.

In reviewing his page, I find some solace in the fact that in no way does Facebook replicate who this man is in real life. I do not believe that it could. And that's the point I'm making here about Facebook. My friend is an exceedingly talented and richly multifarious type of guy. I highly value the conversations we have in person. There are many things in life that we share a common point of view on, and the things we do see differently, we would never let stand in the way of our friendship. Just as with my wife's Facebook page, his Facebook page does not reflect his true personality. And it would be impossible for this website or any social media site to do so.

There is, however, something that Facebook and nearly any other social media site can do for you. They can cause you distress, negativity, and depression. How so? Scientists argue that the hugely popular social networking sites exert an emotional spillover effect that may carry significant consequences for an increasingly interconnected world. I don't know how they analyze this crap, and quite frankly, I don't care. I'm no scientist, but here's what I get from their findings. Imagine what it's like being in a room full of people happily socializing and having a good time. Someone walks into the room carrying some pretty dark energy, and nearly everyone in the room senses it. While likely not even realizing why, most of the people in the room have their positive attitude and happy socializing taken down at least a notch or two. If the person who entered is dark and negative enough, he or she could easily wreck the positive situation the socializers found themselves in before the person entered. The way I see it, the same thing can happen to you in a social media situation. Can you guard yourself from all the negative crap floating around on Facebook and other social media sites? Hell no. It's everywhere. But you sure as heck can put up your shields and not let this negative crap stick to you. You should. And if you don't know how, it would benefit you to learn pretty quickly.

Twitter comes in at number two with over 200 million active users and 500 million accounts. That's a lot of tweets. Twitter is still claiming to be in the number two slot even though Google+ claims

343 million active users. My guess is the first liar for social media supremacy doesn't have a chance. MySpace supposedly comes in at number four with LinkedIn in fifth. Then comes Orkut, Friendster, Hi5, Bebo, and Netlog rounding out the top ten. This data comes from the Toptenreviews.com website. The data might as well be coming from the sacred scrolls no more than I understand it. But let's take a closer look at number two: Twitter.

    It sounds a bit odd telling you this, but Twitter is a website I actually enjoy and have an appreciation for. Not a true understanding, mind you, but I appreciate the site nonetheless. This is because I feel much more in control on Twitter than I do on Facebook. The first reason being that even though they may have promoted tweets, it's not nearly as annoying or distracting as the blatant in-your-face sponsored advertising on Facebook. On Twitter you follow only the people you choose to follow, and I must make some reasonably intelligent choices because the people I follow put up some reasonably intelligent tweets. I don't even find the retweets annoying because they usually contain some content that will interest me and that I may benefit from. Of course, the Twitter feeds I follow are people I admire. Mostly entrepreneurs, authors, investigative journalists not tied to the mainstream media, businesses in my coaching niche, and a few crazy-good famous chefs thrown in for my culinary interests. People like author Susan Cain, *@susancain*, who reinforces for me that it really is OK to just be myself and take full advantage of exactly who I am. People like Gerald Celente, *@geraldcelente*, whose tweets constantly remind me to deal in the facts and think for myself. Gerald dishes up a large dose of reality, accept it or not, and also shows me many ways to spot future trends. Or Chef Edward Lee, *@chefedwardlee*, who reminds me that I can be a more adventurous chef in the kitchen, possibly without poisoning my family and friends. Or one of my favorites, Greg Palast, *@greg_palast,* who not only investigates what's really going on in this crazy-ass world but also documents it and publishes it.

I find the Twitter feeds of people like these to be educational; informing; and, many times, inspiring. Because of their activity on the Twitter website, I am a better informed businessman, a more humble person, and feel better connected to humankind. I choose not to follow any celebrity Twitter feeds, sports stars, political pundits, organizations, or anyone else tweeting anything I feel would not be of value to me. But that's just me of course. Twitter also gives me a sense of power at times when someone I'm following comes down with an acute case of tweeting diarrhea and starts spewing out tweets like crap through a goose. On Twitter I had to learn how to unfollow someone early on. Click on the person's name, click the unfollow button, and you're out of here. The glorious feeling of social media supremacy. Obviously, this is the reason the Twitter social media website is a favorite of mine, but what about the social media junkie?

This is where things begin to get real nauseating. Not the website mind you, but the mindlessly tweeting social media junkies who use it. As I'm writing this, according to the website Twittercounter.com, the top five Twitter feeds with the most followers are currently Justin Bieber, Katy Perry, Lady Gaga, Barack Obama, and Taylor Swift. It appears many active users on the Twitter website are not into this form of social media for anything even remotely intellectually fulfilling. Justin Bieber at number one. Are you kidding me? Not only that, but according to the Twitter website, this little dork of a celeb has over forty-two million followers of his Twitter feed. Some simple grade school math will quickly show you that according to the numbers, nearly one in four active users on the Twitter website are hanging on Mr. Bieber's every tweet. So let's take a look at what the forty-two million or so find so damn riveting with this Twitter feed and what might be learned there.

Is It Safe To Friend a Dead Guy on Facebook?

    First of all I hope this kid is paying his social media army generously. He can afford to, and according to his feed, they have sent out 22,857 tweets. I'm grateful that I do not feel like less of a man with my 486. OK, so what might we find to be intellectually stimulating in his nearly 23,000 tweets to the forty-two mill? Here's one: "Gotta get some rest before the show." Brilliant. We wouldn't want poor Justin passing out on stage. How about another one: "LOL." That's it. Nothing else to say in his tweet. Maybe he was laughing out loud when he discovered his followers had rolled past the forty-two million mark. Here's another tweet that took a lot of thought: "Amazing day!" He might be onto something with this one. I find it totally amazing that forty-two million Twitter users would actually follow this crap. I must give some credit to his social media and marketing team though. Many of his tweets offer links to drive his followers to various websites selling his swag. With over forty-two million on the feed, it should not be very difficult to pick up a little extra lunch money for the star. Damn, I love capitalism. The conscious free-market type. Not the crony capitalism bullshit being forced upon free markets globally. Just thought I'd clarify that.

I found another telling number in a very popular Twitter feed. That being the fourth most popular—Barack Obama, the president of the United States. According to the Twitter Counter website, the pres currently has 34.3 million followers. Yet in the 2012 election, he received 65.9 million of the popular votes. This leads me to a question. If Barack Obama is so good at attracting voters to the booth, why can't he kick Justin Bieber's ass on Twitter? Come on now, Mr. President. Kick it up a notch, would you? In less than ten million more followers, you can become the king of Twitter. But if you look at the content on the president's Twitter feed, you will rapidly realize why Justin has the president's ass in a sling. The president has ninety-five hundred tweets and over nine thousand of them are lies. Excuse me—that may have been politically incorrect. And over nine thousand of them obviously misspoken. There, that's better. It appears the president's social media staff is proficient at spreading the bullshit around. Lie to them enough times, and maybe they will believe it.

Now let's take a look at Twitter junkies that hold the record for sending out the most tweets. The first four most tweetable feeds come from Japan with the fifth being from Venezuela. Could this be a cultural thing? Apparently so, and I'm sure some cultural psychologist out there is aware of the compelling reason why. I, on the other hand, can only surmise that Japanese Twitter junkies also happen to be the biggest assholes. Number one by a landslide has sent out nearly 36.5 million tweets. The thing I find fascinating is that this Twitter feed has over thirty-six thousand followers and is following nearly the same amount of other feeds. My guess is they are not doing this from a smartphone. I could be wrong. Number two, also from Japan, has sent out over 7 million tweets. Yet there are only twenty-six followers on this Twitter feed with only fifteen being followed. Over 7 million? To twenty-six people? Need I say more?

The number three and number four most popular social media websites are allegedly Google+ and MySpace. Neither of these are going to make my radar in this book because, quite frankly, I do not know a thing about them, and at this point in my life, I do not intend to know a thing about them. If you would care to go to this book's website at Deadguyonfacebook.com and provide me with a compelling reason why I should include these two in the next edition of this book, I'll definitely consider it. But for now I do not have the time or the desire to do so, although I am confident they are filled with social media junkies.

So let's discuss number five on the list, LinkedIn, a website I am familiar with. About ten years ago, I was meeting with a business friend of mine, and he asked me if I had created a page for myself on the LinkedIn website yet. On what website? I had no idea what he was talking about. So he told me about this website, designed for business people and professional networking, and how important it was for me to have my profile on it. Really? At that time I had been in business for thirty years, was doing just fine, and could not imagine having my profile on some website that I'd never heard of provide me with a benefit for my business in any way. I did, however, greatly respect my business friend, so I made a note and within a week created a business profile of myself on LinkedIn. After doing so I promptly forgot about it for a number of years. Fast forward to early 2013.

A young lady I had done business with previously in one of my other ventures contacted me by e-mail to let me know there was a big discussion going on about me and my business-coaching services on a LinkedIn group. She wanted to let me know she had chimed in on the group, singing praises about my knowledge and abilities and the wonderful experience she'd had doing business with me in the past. I shot her back a reply thanking her for contacting me and providing me with the business testimonial on LinkedIn, but, at least at this point, I really had no idea what she was talking about. But she had gotten my attention, and I intended to find out.

That weekend I blocked some time at home exclusively to going on the LinkedIn site, locating what she had addressed in her e-mail, and updating my profile while I was there. It didn't take me long to realize how much the LinkedIn website had evolved since I'd last been there and how useful it might prove itself to be in my current business. But first I took to updating my business profile on the website. My current businesses were out of date. My business experience could use several additions to it. Even the head shot in my profile was dated, considering I had dropped fifty pounds since the one on the site had been taken.

As a side note, in case you're curious, considering the amount of obesity in the developed world now, I only needed to do two things to drop nearly 18 percent of my body weight and keep it off. The first thing I did was hook up with a fitness guru by the name of Matt Furey. A man I'm now proud to call my friend. Matt's training is global, so feel free to Google him if you could stand to drop a few pounds. Many of his valuable mind-body connection products are available on his website at mattfurey.com. The second thing I did, thanks to a suggestion from Matt, was to quit drinking any kind of sodas and lay off anything containing high-fructose corn syrup. That's it—those two things. Fifty pounds, gone, zip.

Anyway, the LinkedIn profile picture showed a corpulent business guy, and it no longer fit the bill. I do hope some will benefit from my sidetracking though. Maybe the guy who purchased the *FatBurner 2K* app for his smartphone.

After updating my profile, I found that the website had added a number of useful business groups, formerly known as Internet chat boards, and I set about searching for the discussion about my business services. Thanks to the well-organized site, it didn't take me long to locate it. In the business group I located, a small-business owner had inquired about the business-information products and services I offer to the industry and my clients. Much to my surprise, a number of my clients were familiar with the LinkedIn site and were also participants in a number of the business groups on the site. They all sang high praises, through my eyes much higher than what I deserved, about the information and services I had provided to them and how greatly their business had benefited because of mine. I spotted opportunity on LinkedIn.

Turns out the businessman who'd originally asked the question about me on the LinkedIn group became a client of mine because of the replies he'd received from a few of my clients. Since then I've received many new leads and several additional clients exclusively through LinkedIn without pimping any of my wares. I just provide sensible answers to questions posted in the business groups I'm on, all the time knowing that if these business people feel I provide enough value, they will seek out my service. So it turns out that LinkedIn is beneficial to my business and monetizes well for me without eating up a bunch of my work time, but are there business social media junkies in this world wasting their life on LinkedIn? Of course there are. Let's take a little broader look at the LinkedIn website.

One of the first things I noticed when updating my profile on the website was toward the bottom there were a number of people who'd endorsed me for certain things I'd done in business. These endorsements, under the heading of skills and expertise, were unsolicited. Entrepreneurship, marketing, management, coaching, sales, business development: all are things I have done for most of my adult life. Wait a minute. Three people endorsed me for telecom

BSS. What the hell is that? I know what telecom is because I've had business phones on numerous occasions. I also know that BSS generally stands for business support systems. I hope in this case it does not stand for bullshit systems. Besides, who are these people who endorsed me and felt I had an expertise in telecom business support systems? I clicked on the little tab to find out. OK, I know these three people, but why in the world would they ever endorse me for telecom BSS? This is a business system I've always been willing to write the check for to outsource it.

So how popular are these LinkedIn endorsements, and do they really carry any weight in your profile? Upon further research I came to the conclusion these endorsements are nothing more than a bucket of fluff in your LinkedIn profile. Total bull when it comes down to true business acumen and possibly nothing more than propping up one's plump business ego. I came to this conclusion upon discovering that LinkedIn CEO, Jeff Wiener, trumpeted the new endorsement product, hitting one billion endorsements in just under five months after LinkedIn added endorsements. One billion mindless clicks with zero true value to be found in this hot, steamy, and smelly pile of endorsement mania. That's good.

According to the LinkedIn website, the most followed profile is currently the president of the United States, Barack Obama, who is quickly closing in on one million followers. On visiting the president's profile, I could not glean one bit of information about him that I wasn't already aware of. At least his social media team saw fit to throw in a few links driving his LinkedIn followers to his personal web pages. I was also relieved to discover that his LinkedIn profile did not contain the endless stream of crap spewing out of his Twitter feed. I left his profile with only one question bouncing around in my head. I wonder if the president of the United States is in any way troubled by the fact that he has exactly zero endorsements on his LinkedIn profile?

With social media exploding like Joey Chestnut's colon after a Nathan's hot dog eating contest, it was only a matter of time until some software programmers and developers would take a stab at providing the social media junkies with some digital backbone. One such software application, simply entitled *Freedom,* is billed as an Internet blocking productivity software. On Freedom's website at Macfreedom.com, the application is explained thusly:

> Freedom is an amazing little app for Windows and Mac computers that locks you away from the net for up to eight hours at a time. At the end of your time off-line, freedom allows you back on the Internet. Freedom enforces freedom; you'll need to reboot if you want to get back online while Freedom's running. The hassle of rebooting means you're less likely to cheat, letting you focus on work.

Could social media junkies really be serious about installing and running the *Freedom* application on their devices? Only time will tell, but the mere existence of this type of application is cause for hope.

What if you try the *Freedom* app and find out that instead of causing you to be more productive, it's causing you to be an even bigger idiot by wasting time rebooting your computer every time you need your Internet fix? Then you may want to consider an application that provides you with an even bigger and stronger pair of digital family jewels. It's an application called *Cold Turkey*, located at Getcoldturkey.com. All you do is download it, set it, and forget it. Yet *Cold Turkey* does not forget you. You can choose to temporarily block social media sites, games, programs, and any other time-wasting digital junk you may find yourself addicted to. Just pick the programs and sites; choose the length of time you want to block them, anywhere from ten minutes to an entire month; and tell the app you are ready to go cold turkey. Your distractions are no longer accessible to anyone using that computer. Not only that, but unlike *Freedom, Cold Turkey* survives the reboot. Talk about a severe digital withdrawal for many.

Of course, if you're a serious social media junkie who chooses to give *Freedom* a try so you can actually accomplish something meaningful at your computer or device, your addiction will likely cause you pain and struggle while the *Freedom* app is running. After all, you're trying to accomplish some work with no social media, no e-mail, no instant messaging (IMs), and not even a few websites operating in additional Windows. You may find your mind wandering out to the most efficient means of self extermination. OK, give in and reboot your computer before you start doing some really stupid things. When the Internet springs back to life though, go immediately to your search engine of choice and look up the *Rescue Time* software application available on the net.

Available at Rescuetime.com, this software app is more like a digital nanny while the *Freedom* app is more like an Internet prison guard. *Rescue Time* does not block your ability to do anything you choose on your digital devices. What it does do (kind of like the NSA here in the United States) is track everywhere you go and everything you do and also the amount of time you spend doing it. Eventually guilting you enough to supposedly change your ways, to quit wasting so many precious hours at some of the most stupid places in your digital life. Could the hard data from the *Rescue Time* app have a positive effect on a social media junkie? Honestly, I don't know. But I do know this. Hard data, especially hard business data, can have a profoundly positive effect on you when it is telling you that you're doing something really wrong or really stupid. Occasionally, the facts will get in the way of the stupidity. At least it has in my life. So I have to believe that the hard data from this application could at least show you the error in your ways.

The app's website states the following:

> Rescue Time is an automatic time and attention tracker that helps individuals and teams propagate good processes and eliminate bad habits. Fight information overload and multitask thrash! Measure your call time and mobile app use time to manage your digital life for business and productivity. New users will get a lifetime free individual web account when activating your app. All new users also get fourteen days of pro web reporting mode, which then reverts to the free mode (still very popular!) until upgraded from our site. Be sure to try the desktop/laptop app too. One account is all you need for as many devices as you have.

Just think of the possibilities. One simple app giving you documented proof of how big an asshole you are being in your digital life and how much of your day goes completely wasted because of your social media addiction. You can even share this documented time abuse with all of your friends on Facebook! I would not, however, suggest sharing hard *Rescue Time* data with your employer for obvious reasons. That is, unless you wish to quickly turn him or her into your former employer. With more and more applications appearing regularly to help increase your productivity on your devices and hopefully help you break your social media addiction, could it be that the people who helped cause your addiction to be possible, digital device programmers, are starting to feel guilty about your addiction and trying to assist you to wean you off your fixation with digital crap? I doubt it, but at least it's a positive thought.

There are, of course, many additional social media sites available to anyone with a device and an Internet connection. With the rapid growth of social networking, there are a growing number of social media junkies who may feel that sites like Facebook are too mainstream for their liking. They do not need to look far to find additional social networks catered more to their individual tastes and interests. Alternatives abound from the strange and sketchy to the curiously niche. For instance, true social media zombies may choose to gravitate to the lost-zombies social network. Located at Lostzombies.com, the creators describe the site as "a zombie themed social network whose goal is to create a community generated zombie movie." Who knew? Probably even less enlightening, who cares? Although I suspect that the community-generated movies created could prove to be a huge hit for zombie lovers. After all, it takes one to make one.

There are social media sites exclusively for dog lovers, cat lovers, horse lovers, even hamster lovers. But if you would like to take a step outside of the pet community, how about an exclusive social media site for vampire lovers? The social media website located at Vampirefreaks.com is described by *The Huffington Post* thusly: "The creator of vampire freaks initially used the site to post photos and industrial music reviews. The site eventually grew into a subculture community. Users can now create profiles and join 'cults' devoted to bands, haircuts, iconic figures, etc." Sounds like the perfect medium to me to find out about the latest vampire events or to host your next Gothic party.

There are some social media websites designed to bring different types of people together in order to accomplish a main purpose. Like a complimentary boob job. Seriously. If you take your browser to Myfreeimplants.com, you will find the site described as "a social networking website that provides a fun, safe, and debt-free alternative to expensive breast augmentation loans." I wonder if the Hooters restaurant chain is behind this website. The site describes that its community is comprised of three groups of people. The first group obviously being women who are dissatisfied for some reason with their bustline yet are not in the position to pony up the bucks to the plastic surgeon to do something about it. The poor things—living with small boobs and an even smaller checking account balance.

On the website the thought of a free boob job is seductively sold to these ladies, stating that thanks to the site they can get curves they've always dreamed of with a free breast augmentation. They can also safely network with benefactors online and earn donations to help them achieve their cosmetic surgery goals. The site goes on to promise they will make friends, earn donations, and have fun while learning at their own pace. It says there are no loans, no interest, and nothing to pay off. They should choose to set their own goals, set their own limits, and even select their preferred plastic surgeon. They are promised that they are in complete control. If they were in complete control of their digital lives, would they truly seek out this website? Sorry, that was a rhetorical question.

The second group on this website is a group of people referred to as "Contributors." Seeking contributions, the website promises to allow these contributors to "help the women of your dreams achieve the body of their dreams." A lofty goal indeed. The website goes on to promise that with their contributions and support, they can play an active role in helping the women reach their goals while developing connections that last a lifetime. They can also interact virtually with any of the four-thousand-plus active flat-chested women seeking their friendship and assistance. They can choose to contribute with direct donations of any amount and receive photos, videos, messages, and everlasting gratitude in exchange. Can you imagine?

Betty, who's that guy that keeps texting you?

Oh, that's my former online friend Bob. We met on a website where he helped finance my boob job, but now he's turned into a creeper and actually wants to see them. No boob for Bob, at least not in my lifetime.

Poor Bob.

The third group on this website, predictably so, are plastic surgeons. These knife-wielding, silicone-schlepping cosmetic creepers are obviously on this website for one specific reason. Someone needs to be there who is willing to take the contributions of the second group in order to fulfill the perceived needs of the first group. The boob sculptors are promised they will reach a vast network of potential clients looking for quality plastic surgeons. With over eight million page views per month, no other cosmetic surgery website can put their practice in front of more qualified leads. As of this writing, there are 323 cosmetic surgeons signed up and listed on the site. Let's see, 323 docs and over four thousand women actively seeking their services. Lots of work available if we can find the contributors.

Yet with the typical surgery listed on the site averaging $5,500, it appears we are asking these contributors to pony up some twenty-two million bucks. Is the result of four thousand pairs of bigger boobs really worth the cost? Evidently so because the website proclaims to have 750-plus success stories of women who have transformed their bustline appearance thanks to the generosity of the contributors on the site. Bless their hearts. I wonder if it's tax deductible. Somehow I just can't find it in my heart to ask my CPA about that one.

There are digital communities online in the form of social networks that cater to nearly every person's interest, hobby, or obsession that you can imagine. Many of them quite predictable, relating to business, religion, politics, and chosen lifestyles. Yet there are some social networks dedicated to passions that most would have a difficult time of even justifying the existence of the digital community, let alone the passion involved. One such social site struck me this way when I discovered there was a social media network and membership site dedicated to bad haircuts. One bad haircut in particular. This happened when I stumbled upon Mulletpassions.com. I'm not making this up. The website touts itself as being a 100-percent-free social networking and online dating site specifically for singles with a mullet, and for those with the taste and style to appreciate these unique trendsetters. You are instructed to browse the "mullet groups" section to find members based on the style of their mullet: classic, mud flap, or spiky. Who knew?

By the way, I'm not in any way suggesting that you visit Mulletpassions.com either now or in the future, and if you choose to do so, I am in no way responsible for any digital brain damage or emotional distress it may cause you. Consider yourself warned.

Moving on to some higher goals in social media, have you ever considered participating in an online community to learn more about where your soul might land in the afterlife? Me either. But if this is something that interests you, there is a social media site at Lineforheaven.com that promises to do just that. Not only that but the religious social media site claims it will assist you in getting all of your spiritual ducks in a row before you go off to meet your maker. Could this website really make me a better person if I belong to it while I'm still among the living? Let's see, here's what the website claims:

> Lineforheaven.com helps answer the fundamental question, "Am I going to Heaven?" and proves its slogan "Religion can be fun!" The first religion-based Web 2.0 site in history, lineforheaven is open to all religious views and feels anyone should be able to get into Heaven, i.e. no one will be denied entry on basis of religion. The only requirement is to do good deeds. Unlike any other website, lineforheaven.com gives you the ability to save your "Soul" and reserve a place in "Heaven" by earning Karma Points. Those with the most Karma Points are deemed most worthy and may earn a chance to become closer to "God." Why waste your time on other sites, meeting creepy strangers, when you could get closer to "God" on our site? Join the new earth shattering social gathering that promotes religious tolerance through fun and games. All religious views are welcome, your privacy is guaranteed, and it takes only a minute to sign up for free. And for good cause!

OK, I understand at least a few things about this website's description. Becoming a more spiritual individual and going through your life carrying out good deeds, the desire to be a caring person and open to the things around you in this lifetime, and through your actions at least feeling as if you're closer to God. I also get the karma thing. As you likely know, karma can be a good thing or a real bitch. But karma points? Why wasn't I taught about this as a young boy in my catechism class? Were the nuns holding out on my karma points so they could keep them for themselves? I guess that doesn't matter now. If I've learned anything in this lifetime, it's how to collect my own karma points, and I certainly don't need a religious social media site to do so. I hope you don't either.

I've got to end this chapter on social media junkies by discussing with you a small online social community it's likely you and I will

never participate in. There is a social site called A Small World located at Asmallworld.com. It's an invitation-only social network that relaunched in the spring of 2013 as a by-invitation, members-only travel and lifestyle club with a capped membership of 250,000 members. This social media website presents itself as the definitive answer of how to separate the world's ultra-affluent global elitist types from the unwashed masses in social media. Interesting. Could this website be the anti-Facebook? Let's take a look. The landing page on the website states the following:

> Membership in ASW is by invitation only, which creates and protects the trust and authenticity that make ASW comfortable and stand out. If you know someone with invitation privileges, you can ask them to invite you. If not, please be patient and continue to ask around in your own personal and professional circles.

To paraphrase Groucho Marx, what immediately comes to mind for me is "I don't care to belong to any club that would have me as a member!"

But let's dig a little deeper into this ASW thing. Even if we qualified financially and socially for ASW membership, would it really be worth our while to be only one click away from aristocracy, celebrities, and supermodels? I suppose it would depend on how much you value the contact with these members. For me personally, I'll stick with Groucho's comment. I did however find one thing very favorable on the ASW website even though Satan would be wearing long underwear before I'm a member. That thing is the website also has a foundation. Site data includes the following:

> Founded in 2004, a small world relaunched in the spring of 2013 as the leading international travel and

lifestyle club with an emphasis on community, charity, and collective travel wisdom from the very best source—the well-traveled. Membership is comprised of people united by a common sensibility and sense of purpose: to seek out the extraordinary and share their experiences with one another. No matter where they go, they open their lives and passports to each other to ensure that they feel a sense of belonging— and feel at home—anywhere in the world. The Asmallworld Foundation was created to harness that spirit of selflessness that our members all share. By leveraging the power of our global network—and partnering with a growing list of leading international charities—the ASWF will address today's most dire issues in global health, education, and women's rights in developing countries.

Amen to that one. Those in the world possessing an obscene amount of assets should be able to choose where all of their excess will do the most good in the world. And I thank them for that.

Who is our next target? People who are addicted to something I actually know very little about. But I felt it was worthy of giving them a mention. Video game junkies.

Video Game Junkies

OK, let me get this straight. You're twenty-eight years old and hold a college degree in criminal psychology. You're up to your ass in school loans, and you've just lost your job as a retail associate at OfficeMax due to the economy. Because of your situation, you've moved back in with your divorced mom because she didn't want to see you living like a homeless person. You've submitted nearly thirty resumes, the kind they teach you how to effectively design in college, in the past three months, and you have yet to get an interview for employment. And because you are bored, you spend most of your time in your formerly happy mother's house either sleeping or playing video games.

Think I made this scenario up? I can pretty much guarantee you that at least someone who is currently reading the previous paragraph is shaking his or her head and saying, *Oh my God. He wrote this chapter about my son!* Think I'm kidding? The percentage of adult children still living with their parents has ballooned in the past few years. In some places over 50 percent of them are pilfering at least one parent out of their much-deserved privacy. And it doesn't appear this trend is going to change anytime soon. With global governments waging a big war on small business, the real job creators in this world have zero incentive and no sane reasons to increase the work force in their businesses one iota.

But I have strayed off course here. Let's get back to the video game junkies.

Before you begin calling me just some crazy old fart, let's get one thing perfectly clear. I understand games. I grew up playing cards, shooting darts, and lying about made up words on a Scrabble board. I was actually born playing poker. Figuratively speaking. My mother gave birth to me in the early morning on New Year's Day. While she was playing poker at the family New Year's Eve party, she was also timing her labor pains and telling the other players approximately how many more hands could be played until she had to go to the hospital. I'm not kidding here, but don't worry. I was her third child, and she was also a registered nurse. No child abuse here—I was in good hands. My father, on the other hand, started out being pissed at his only son. Not only was I delivered at a time that broke up the New Year's Eve poker game, but I also cheated him out of an entire year's tax deduction by just a little over three hours. Sorry, Dad. It wasn't my choice.

But the games I grew up playing required a different skill set than just the hand-eye coordination I'm assuming is required to play video games. Shooting darts on a real dartboard required math, muscle memory, social skills, and usually a few beers. Playing cards successfully required a thorough knowledge of the game and the ability to read the other players' body language. Poker taught me at a young age how to effectively manage risk. A skill that would prove to be extremely valuable in my entrepreneurial life. And Scrabble was always challenging me to greatly expand my vocabulary. Besides, most of the time I played Scrabble with family members; therefore, all the swear words I knew were out of bounds. Even the ones in Polish and Italian. Damn it.

But what is the video game industry contributing to our children's future? From what I can see, not much, unless your kids go on to become video game industry moguls. It's likely, however, that will never happen because they'll be too damn glued to their video game controller to ever even think about picking up a book and learning something about business. I realize these things are supposed to be an electronic form of entertainment, but what real skill sets and knowledge are the video games actually providing to our kids? I couldn't answer that question when writing this chapter because I have honestly never played a video game in my life, unless you consider a video poker machine in a casino to be a video game.

I do not, and here's why. Video poker games require an in-depth knowledge of odds and probabilities. Effectively playing video poker without putting yourself in the poorhouse requires a math skill set far beyond what most people are willing to learn. Learning to identify which cards to hold for the highest probability of a return is something most players do not have the discipline to do. And being able to spot how the casinos vary the payoffs of certain hands gives you the ability to accurately calculate the exact percentage of advantage the casino has over the player. This all may sound to you like I just removed any entertainment factor from video poker, but to me it just adds to the entertainment factor. Why is that? Winning may be fun, but I really hate losing.

So because I could not answer what sort of social contribution the video game industry may be making, or not, to our future generations, I had to turn to the Internet. I went to the Omgtoplists.com website and located a list of the ten most popular video games for 2013. Stick with me on this one because I feel this is mighty telling. Coming in at number ten is a video game called *ZombiU*. On the cover? A picture of a zombie man in a hat with the flesh hanging off his face and blood dripping down his chin and his eyes cast in a fixed state of horror. His mouth hanging open in screaming terror as if he had just eaten his smartphone. I sure hope the poor zombie creep doesn't get indigestion.

A brief description on the website of the game states the following:

> A zombie outbreak occurs in London and the player has to survive thanks to their wits rather than by going on a zombie killing rampage. Once your character dies it will become a zombie and you might face it with your new character. *ZombiU* is an interesting alternative to the traditional zombie games.

So what might the kiddies learn from being glued to the *ZombiU* set for any number of given hours? One thing I quickly noted is the game actually gives them a choice not to go on a killing rampage. A good thing I would think. The game description also boldly states that no matter what you do in the game, your character will die. Maybe that's a quick lesson in no such thing as immortality. It may even teach them a skill set on how to deal with digital zombies in real life if they ever break their video game addiction. Think about the title to that kid's book: *How I Went from Being a Video Game Junkie to a Digital Zombie Psychologist*. Could be a bestseller.

Let's jump to number six on the list: a game billed as *Far Cry 3*. The cover sports a photo of a gent who appears to be in a tropical setting. He's a survivalist-looking dude sporting a black mohawk and a big scar on his forehead. His right hand contains a semiautomatic pistol, and there is a knife strapped to his right bicep. He has a sober and determined look on his face. Might have something to do with the two bodies hanging behind him in the background. The description of the game states the following:

> You will find yourself stranded in a tropical island where you quickly have to adapt in order to survive. The story is well-developed and you will meet a lot of interesting characters. This game is very immersive and you will have a hard time taking a break from it.

OK, at least we're not outwitting any zombies in this one that I know of. But I really can't, for the life of me, spot any practical knowledge little Johnny might pick up here unless he is eventually in the position to need survival skills. At least the description issues a clear warning that playing this video game will turn into a long drawn-out time suck. Thanks for the warning. The description also promises that you will meet a lot of interesting characters. How refreshing. If you really want to meet some interesting characters, how about getting your head out of the video console and doing a little charity work in your community? Nah, I didn't think so. You are most likely a far cry from even considering stopping playing *Far Cry 3*.

At number one is a video game simply called *Dishonored*. The cover is a picture of some Viking-appearing dude looking down at his knife during a rainstorm and wearing some sort of skull and crossbones suit of armor. Actually, a look that would go quite well at my next costume party. The games description states the following:

> Your character has been framed for a murder he did not commit and you have to get out of this bad situation by making the right decisions. Every decision you make will impact the storyline. You can play the game more than once and the scenario will always be different. You can choose two modes to defeat your enemies: stealth or combat. *Dishonored* is one of the best games available at the moment

since you can easily turn the storyline into your own adventure thanks to the many choices you will be faced with.

Number one huh?

OK, I actually like the thing about getting out of a bad situation by making the right decisions. Although, without ever seeing this game, I can easily predict that any decisions you may make in this video game, you will never face in real life. The description also begs some sort of shelf life for the game because of the different scenarios available in it. Number one may even hold the video game junkie's attention until *Dishonored 2* comes out. I assume that's what the developer is hoping for. You are even offered two modes to defeat your enemies: stealth or combat. If you ever pry yourself away from your video game console and get out in the real world and make some real enemies, I predict you will be scrambling to look for any modes offered to defeat them. Good luck with that.

So it may be useful to look at just how hooked the average video game junkie can be. Well, according to the website Internetaddictiondisorder.org, it depends on whether the gamers are playing the average off-line video game or the average online computer game. Whereas the average off-line video game player plays an average of six hours per week, the average online computer game player plays around twenty-five hours per week. A clear two-thirds of these addicts are under the age of thirty, and currently, the average person afflicted with computer game addiction is expected to have a total of two years playing computer games by the age of thirty. I will give one thing to the average addict. Video game junkies spend approximately as much time playing their games as it would take for them to study to earn a degree in worthlessness in college, but without the mountain of student debt. Yet, my guess on this observation would be the majority of them are actually doing both. Two degrees in worthlessness. All the qualifications needed to be a government employee.

Of course, these very general video game junkie statistics only apply to gaming on a video console or gaming on one's computer. What about gaming on your smartphone? Smartphone games come in more colors than the 120-count crayons in a Crayola super selection box, and the smartphone games will not melt when left out in the sunshine. Some of the smartphone games are so ridiculous they defy description. Here's a new game for your Android as described by Yannick LeJacq of NBC news:

> Are you a fan of disruptive technology? Well, there's a new mobile app that's so disruptive it may actually break your smartphone.
>
> That's the idea behind *Send Me to Heaven,* a new mobile sport game whose main objective involves hurling your phone as high in the air as humanly possible.
>
> Apparently, the idea of chucking a handheld device that costs more than a month's rent toward the heavens for the purpose of fun was too much for Apple, and according to the game's developers, the company rejected it before it ever had the chance to enter the iOS App Store and send so many chamfered edges rocketing toward the celestial bodies.
>
> As Apple reportedly put it to the developers, *"Send Me to Heaven* was rejected for encouraging behavior that could result in damage to the user's device." In the postjackass era, that's practically a sales pitch.

Luckily enough for Android phone owners who still wish to void their warranty, *Send Me to Heaven* is available for free on Google Play. Yes, this game is free to play. I think I finally understand what my economics professor meant when he kept saying, "There ain't no such thing as a free lunch."

To the game's credit, however, the scoring system monitors exactly how high the phone goes, thereby turning *Send Me to Heaven* into what theoretically sounds like a high-altitude game of chicken. All players compete to see who is willing to take the risk to chuck their phone the extra ten feet to get a high score (no pun intended). I'd just really prefer not to be the guy who loses, or the one who wins for that matter.

Can you imagine being enough of a video game junkie to start throwing your device straight up and hopefully catching it on the way back down? If you would ever be a big enough idiot to try this game, one can only hope your mobile device would come down and hit you on the head, knocking some sense into you. Let's take a look at some of the more popular mobile video games that do not require you to give your device a pitch. There's a popular one that was released in May of 2013 called *Plague Inc.* A description of the game states the following:

> You'd think that a game featuring the travel path of a viral plague would be dead boring, but Ndemic Creations proves that a game that's essentially a spreadsheet simulation of a deadly viral plague across the globe is compelling entertainment. It has

no fancy 3-D graphics, cut scenes, or voice work, just a map of the world, several choices about how to best spread the disease most effectively (Rats? Air Travel? Mosquitoes?), and a well-built simulation of how the world responds to your pandemic infection. It's a chilling and realistic look at how disease can and does spread from place to place.

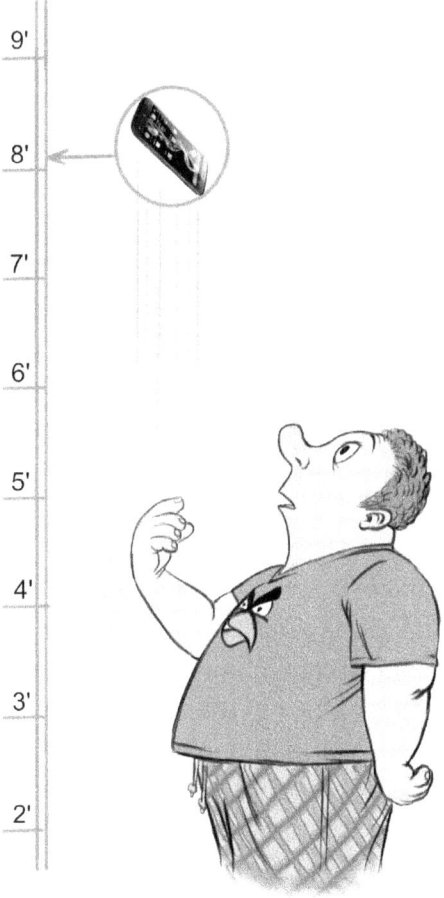

My, what a socially redeeming video game. And you can play it on the run. Spreading your own deadly viral plague across the globe. I have a feeling the only disease that's being spread here is from your mobile device playing *Plague Inc.* to the center of your brain, causing you to stare at your device and drool uncontrollably.

Another very popular mobile video game, released in November 2012, answers the question, what do you get when you cross an idiotically popular video game with a far-out space-themed movie? I believe the answer to this question is *Angry Birds Star Wars*. And that would make the game an idiotically popular far-out space-themed mobile video game. The description of this one cracks me up:

> Rovio Entertainment somehow put two of the strongest intellectual properties together into one incredibly lust-worthy combination. *Star Wars* plus *Angry Birds* seems like an odd match, but it hit number one in the iTunes app charts within the first two and a half hours of release. It likely sold a huge number of copies via the Google Play store as well. Who can resist angry birds with light sabers and officially sanctioned *Star Wars* sound effects? No one, that's who.

All I can say is, wow, how irresistible is that? Are you kidding me? The only thing I can picture in my mind is someone gazing at his or her mobile device with the image of Darth Vader with bird feathers hanging out of his mouth. What a compellingly ridiculous waste of time.

If you happen to have one of these unemployed, adult video game junkies residing with you and sucking up all of your hard-earned resources, I can easily suggest a huge favor you can do for this individual. The next time this person temporarily abandons his or her never ending task of trying to outwit the zombies in the latest video quest—it's likely the video game junkie will be going to the bank to cash his or her latest unemployment check—drag all the person's crap to the curb and have the locks changed on the doors. Make sure the video game console is at the bottom of the pile. If you then want to improve the video game junkie's new experience even further, pick up a copy of best-selling author Larry Winget's timeless classic book entitled *You're Broke Because You Want to Be* and put that on the top of the pile. If this person actually takes an initiative to read the book, it will prove to be a great tool to help the person get the crap off the curb and into his or her own humble abode. Good riddance. Come to think of it, there may be a new product idea here for author Winget and a video game company. How about turning the book *You're Broke Because You Want to Be* into a video game? Every twist and turn of the game will find Larry providing the necessary ass kick to the video game junkie, hopefully encouraging the junkie to abandon his or her addiction for an adult life.

If you would happen to actually be one of these unfortunate individuals I described in the first paragraph of this chapter, let me provide you with a blueprint of how to better your situation in life. Your first step will be to cut the power cord away from your video game console, hopefully having enough sense to unplug the thing from the wall first. Take this power cord and throw it in the trash quickly before you have the urge to wrap it around your neck and hang yourself with it. Locate your favorite source of extra energy, such as a cup of coffee, one of those energy drinks, legal or illegal drugs, or even a Snickers bar, and consume as much as your body will tolerate. After that get your ass out into the real world and seek out what you really need in your life. I'm not speaking of a job. You do not really need a job. What you should truly seek out is an income. Knowing the difference between the two will prove to be highly useful as a recovering video game junkie. By the way, college degrees and resumes are not required to locate an adequate income for yourself. Careful thought and tenacious courage are.

Our next victim is a subject I knew little about until a few years ago. But the learning curve happened very rapidly as soon as my teenage daughter received her very first smartphone. Because of this, I felt it important to offer a few personal stories in the next chapter. I hope my wife and my kid are still on speaking terms with me after they read it. And what are we going to discuss? Texting junkies.

Texting Junkies

I must admit to you that until my daughter received her first cell phone in 2007, I did not have a clue about the popularity of sending and receiving text messages on a digital device. It was just something I had never been exposed to. I remember walking into my provider's store with her to add her to my plan and the geeky kid looking at her and asking, "Do you plan to use your new cell phone to text with?" Sure, why not. Little did I know. We signed her up that day with a package including a minimum amount of text message communications included in the plan. Fast-forward thirty days to the next cell phone bill I received in the mail. What? There has got to be an error here. The amount of my cell phone bill that month could have also been a pretty good down payment on a yacht. Was there a mistake, or is this my new teenage cell phone hell? Upon closer examination, hidden within plain sight on the bill were overages I owed due to my teenage daughter's 12,647 text messages.

Seriously? I had to do the math. OK, she usually sleeps about eight hours per day. She spent six hours per day at her high school where her cell phone is at least supposed to be safely tucked away in her locker. Let's factor in two hours per day for personal hygiene, teenage female primping, and stuffing food in her mouth. That leaves fourteen hours per day two days a week and eight hours per day five days a week for her to text. Sixty-eight hours per week to play with her device. Times four weeks, this is a total of 272 hours. So 12,647 messages divided by 272 hours comes to roughly 46.5 texts per hour. Incredible. Considering she is a texting novice, what in the hell is going to happen when she gets good at this?

After much serious contemplation, along with a fair amount of bourbon on the rocks, I managed to stay composed and decided to sleep on the situation before having a meaningful talk with my daughter about her text overages. The next morning, after my daughter went to school, I sat down with my wife to break the news to her about our daughter's indiscretions with her new cell phone. My wife was beyond mortified. Her first thoughts were to dye the child's hair blond and sell her off to the leader of a Third World nation. I reminded my wife that if caught we would both likely be incarcerated for a good length of time, and the kid would be too damn busy texting to even think about paying us a visit in prison. Attempting to calm my wife down, I said that if we went about this properly, we could turn it into a learning experience for our daughter and a lesson in self-control. These words did not necessarily have a calming effect on my wife.

This prompted me to get up and give my wife a kiss and tell her we could discuss our strategy later in the day when I returned from the office. Truth being I felt she needed a little time with herself to attempt to compose and wrap her brain around the news I had delivered. Sure enough, God bless her, she began calling several of the mothers of my daughter's school chums. *Hello, Margaret? I have an interesting question for you. How many texts does your daughter Elaine send and receive in a month? Excuse me, you don't know? Oh, I see. It's called an unlimited plan. All right, it was good to speak with you this morning, and I hope we can get together sometime soon.* After that, five more calls, and five more I don't knows. Oh well, so much for that idea. Could it be that the parents of my kid's friends are also texting junkies?

Is It Safe To Friend a Dead Guy on Facebook?

Meanwhile, in my office, I'm listing several strategies of how I might want to approach this powwow in order to transform it into a lesson in restraint for my girl. Let's see now, how about if we approach it from the angle of if she would spend even one-tenth of the time studying and doing homework as she does texting, she would be acing high school, flying through her grades effortlessly. No, I don't see a compelling reason for her to do this. The only time she's ever really concerned about her grades is when we threatened to send her off to a convent for the rest of her life. Wait, I have another idea. How about explaining to her that if she spent half as much time writing as she did texting, I could have her as a published author on Amazon.com before the end of the year? Wait, this would also prove ineffectual. First, the kid has no interest in books, even though she's surrounded by them in her home environment. Second, I have significant evidence showing that the kid might believe that money *really does* grow on trees. With this belief system, she will never have a yearning to actually earn some of the stuff.

Then a light bulb comes on above my noggin. Let's see, if my kid's friend's parents have no idea how many texts are being sent and received in a one-month period, then my kid will not have a clue either. Why not give her the option to pick a number for what she feels is a reasonable amount of texts to be sent and received per month? Brilliant. This just might work. We will sit down and negotiate what a practical volume of texts per month will be for her in the future. I will then adjust her plan to accommodate this number. And if she goes over that number in a month? Simple. She is then responsible for the charge for the overages. Her life savings could be wiped out in ninety days. Perfect. Now get out of the office, go home, and see if this balloon will float with my wife before the kid gets home.

I was pleased to find my wife felt that the plan I proposed would likely teach our daughter a lesson in restraint and responsibility in short order. Her only concern was that of padding the pockets of my cell phone provider needlessly and slaughtering the kid's piggy bank without even giving the poor thing a blindfold. I addressed my wife's concerns by stating, first, it was our daughter negotiating for the limits on her usage, and, second, if things got out of hand, I would quickly readjust the plan with the provider. We agreed this was the best course of action considering the situation, and I couldn't wait to negotiate with the kid when she got home from school. That is, if I could actually get her full attention by putting her new cell phone out of reach for a few minutes.

I was pleased that my daughter actually powered down her device for our talk. Possibly a silent way of begging for mercy? I explained to her that we would negotiate a reasonable amount of text usage per month, and she would be financially responsible for any overages. She understood, and she started at ten thousand. I started at five thousand, explaining the mindless time waste of the whole thing, and we ended up setting her maximum at eight thousand. I then explained to her that would mean she would need to cut her texting activity by one third in the following month. She agreed and told me that she would be more responsible with her device. I gave her a hug, told her I loved her, and stated it would be wise if she would always keep in mind not to waste so much of her time and, now, her money.

She actually did make an effort, yet over the next three months her overage charges were in the $100 per month range. I changed her cell phone plan in order to help accommodate the overages, and after that three-month $300 hit to her savings account, she seemed to come to the realization that the majority of her social interaction with her friends should not consist of texting on their little screens. After that time she never went above ten thousand texts sent and received in a month. Her actual usage was dropping, albeit slowly. When she turned eighteen, I took her back to my provider, stating it would be a smart thing to get her the device she wanted along with the plan to accommodate her needs, and we would put the plan in her name. Most kids never think about building a credit rating at such a young age, yet this is something I had wanted for her all along. Easy access to credit and the responsibility to use it properly. I'm a proud papa to say that more than two years later and, if I'm not mistaken, three new devices, she is still using her cell phone in a responsible and reasonable manner. Thank God. Having an evil human-sized praying mantis living under my roof could have easily pushed me over the edge.

Although I do not text, I can at least see some usefulness in this form of communication. After all, I own a cell phone, I use e-mail, and texting is similar to combining the two. Or at least it should be. It's been my observation that's not really the case. Because it appears to me the texting junkies in my world utilize texting on their cell phones as a way to replace speaking directly with someone on a person-to-person telephone call. Think I'm kidding? In her book *Alone Together: Why We Expect More from Technology and Less from Each Other*, brilliant author and MIT Professor Sherry

Turkle shares what one young girl interviewed for the book has to say about texting and IMs:

> Texting offers protection. Nothing will get spat at you. You have time to think and prepare what you're going to say, to make you appear like that's just the way you are. There's planning involved, so you can control how you're portrayed to this person, because you're choosing these words, editing it before you send it. When you instant message you can cross things out, edit what you say, block a person, or sign off. A phone conversation is a lot of pressure. You're always expected to uphold it, to keep it going, and that's too much pressure. You have to just keep going. "Oh how was your day?" You're trying to think of something else to say real fast so the conversation doesn't die out.

The following is also from *Alone Together*:

> Technologies live in complex ecologies. The meaning of any one depends on what others are available. The telephone was once a way to touch base or ask a simple question. But once you have access to e-mail, instant messaging, and texting, things change. Although we still use the phone to keep up with those closest to us, we use it less outside this circle. Not only do people say that a phone call asks too much, they worry it will be received as demanding too much. Randolph, a forty-six-year-old architect with two jobs, two young children, and a twelve-year-old son from a former marriage, makes both points. He avoids the telephone because he feels tapped out. It promises more than

I'm willing to deliver. If he keeps his communications to text and e-mail, he believes he can keep it together. He explains, now that there is e-mail, people expect that a call will be more complicated. Not about facts. A fuller thing. People expect it to take time or else you wouldn't have called.

These two passages from Turkle's book along with much more that I've studied and observed confirms my belief that our devices, especially the abuse of these devices, is rapidly changing the ways we communicate with each other. Will our grandchildren even be able to carry on a reasonably intelligent telephone conversation? I don't know. But it's possible that they may not be capable of this, especially growing up with these digital devices from day one. Feeling threatened by an actual live call is one thing, but you have to wonder, what effect will all of this texting and instant messaging have on their in-person communication skills? Is having an effective and meaningful conversation with a person or group in person becoming a lost art? Again, I don't know. I don't get out much. And when I do it's usually for work. Since I work with intelligent business professionals, I don't run into many of the evil human-sized praying mantis types. Even when I speak and do presentations in front of a group of business people, I require, that's right—I said require, everyone in the room to shut off their devices. Am I being unreasonable? I don't think so. I just want their full attention. Is ninety minutes getting to be too much to ask for?

One of the cool things I like about the popularity of texting on a digital device, even though I choose not to personally do it myself, is the fact that this trend is rapidly creating a brand-new language. I've always enjoyed learning about linguistics, although you would not know it by reading this book. This is because I write in a conversational style. But give me a book on phonetics, phonology, morphology, syntax, semantics, and pragmatics, and I'm a happy man who can be self entertained for hours. Yet it appears, at least to me, this new language, the language of texting, contains none of these. This new language is a visual thing and appears to be nothing more than a loosely composed string of acronyms that I am totally unaware of. Just some mutated bowl of alphabet soup displaying itself on the screen of your device. So let's take a look at a few of these.

In viewing a list of these texting acronyms I was fascinated by the education I was receiving. For instance, BURMA, at least I thought, is a country in Southeast Asia officially renamed as the Republic of the Union of Myanmar. Silly me. According to the website *Abbreviations.com,* when you send someone a text containing BURMA, you are actually telling that person to *be upstairs and ready, my angel.* Who knew? Considering the wording, I've got a pretty good idea of what the person texting is asking you to be ready for, but what if you live in a ranch home? Maybe we'll end up bumping bellies on the roof this evening. Lord knows, I hope not.

How about if you received the text CTFD? Again, I didn't have a clue. Although if I received it, I would likely think it was from some fire department in Connecticut. Turns out I'm really overthinking the thing, and trying to make sense of this text acronym isn't a reasonable thing to do. Because if someone sent you the text CTFD what that person is really telling you is to *calm the fuck down.* How do they know I'm not calm? I don't know, but it might be a really great reply to someone that just texted you BURMA. What about getting the text DILLIC? Let me see, maybe some dill ice cream? Nah, considering the nature of some of these acronyms, it's more likely a dildo with a tongue. But what that person texting DILLIC to you is really saying is, *Do I look like I care?* This would be a stupid one to text to me. I wonder what the texting acronym would be for *listen, asshole, not only can I not see you on my device to know if you look like you care, but quite frankly, I couldn't care less whether you care or not.*

When sending this reply, the texting junkie certainly wouldn't reply back with HAND. This is an acronym telling the recipient to *have a nice day.* No thanks, I choose not to. Besides, don't tell me what kind of day to have. ISFB is intended to mean *I'm so frigging bored.* Really? You gotta love it. Some texting junkie so bored out of his or her mind tapping away on his or her digital device, and yet the junkie thinks of you, feeling you two might actually enjoy being bored together. I don't think so. Because if you're that damn bored, you will quickly get a text from me stating LYFE—*left you forever*. Not surprisingly, some of this new language takes things to the extreme. NIFOTC, for instance, is supposed to tell your text recipient that you are *nude in front of the camera*. I'm assuming this text message is accompanied by a picture. But let me ask you this: Anthony Weiner wouldn't happen to be with you now, would he?

Of course, if I did receive the text message NIFOTC and took the time to look at the accompanying image, I may have to quickly reply PMSL, which would tell the model in the buff that I just *pissed myself laughing*. Gee, I hope you're not offended. One I can pretty much guarantee you'll never get from a texting junkie is NIFOTC PSNM because that would mean the sender is *naked in front of the camera with parents sitting next to me*. We can only hope that wouldn't be the case. And no, SFETE does not mean that you have stinky feet. In texting it means you're *smiling from ear to ear*. TMTOWTDI in texting language tells someone *there's more than one way to do it*. It? I don't want to know. And who could imagine that UGLY would mean *understanding generous lovable you*? There seems to be a contradiction here, a huge inconsistency, between the English language and the language of texting. And I thought I knew ugly when I saw it. Maybe I will WHFO or *when hell freezes over*.

Of course, that would be in direct contrast with WTFH, which in texting language means *what the flaming hell*. OK, which is it? Hot or cold? I was floored when I saw in text language WYMM?, which according to the abbreviations website is supposed to mean *will you marry me?* I mean what kind of texting junkie idiot would even attempt to propose via a WYMM? text? Isn't this something better done in person? Hopefully with sincerity and love in your voice? And a big, fat-ass engagement ring might not hurt either.

So where do extreme testing junkies go to mix with like-minded people and flaunt their skills? According to CBS News, they might choose to attend and compete at the LG US National Texting Competition. I can't make this crap up; they meet annually in Times Square in New York City to face off against each other. The competition tests three skills: speed, accuracy, and dexterity. The contestants pass through three rounds, including texting while blindfolded, texting with hands behind their backs, and text blitz where contestants have to copy phrases as fast as possible. The texting competition was originally launched in 2007 and is sponsored by LG electronics. Go figure. In 2012 the top spot in the competition was claimed for a second year in a row by Austin Weirschke, a teenager from Queens, New York, and he walked away with $50,000. How proud must little Austin's mother be? Hopefully, she was savvy enough to take the kid's dough and put it in a medical savings account for him. It's a no-brainer that this kid will eventually need some hand surgery.

Think I'm kidding? Numerous occupational therapists who deal with repetitive stress injuries have already named the affliction *texting thumb*. All the repetitiveness from using your thumbs in this bent position tapping away happily on your device can wind up leaving you with some pretty sore thumbs. Predictably, reported cases of texting thumb are on a steady rise. One wacky entrepreneur sensing a need actually came up with a new workout tool called a Thumbell. That's right. A small sixty-five gram weight device resembling a mini barbell with the curve right in the middle where your thumb goes. I'm sure the biggest obstacle for the Thumbell is trying to train texting junkies to put their devices down long enough to actually use it. I wonder if Austin Weirschke has a pair?

    I realize I'm not painting the prettiest picture of typical texting junkies, and they are usually pretty harmless as they mindlessly tap on their devices, wasting their precious time and also the time of their text recipients. Why should I care? Their activity isn't wasting any of my time or causing me any harm. Yet I would be remiss if I did not include all the times when texting on your device at inappropriate times injures people and even causes death. Texting while driving a car, riding a motorcycle, flying an airplane, and even conducting a passenger train. All of these activities have caused horrible injuries and numerous deaths. So are there really any good answers to this growing problem? If so, I haven't seen them.

Sure, there are some states passing laws making it a moving violation to be tapping away on your device while mashing on the gas pedal. It's something, but this approach really falls short of being a good answer. How easily our legislators forget that you cannot legislate common sense anymore than you can legislate the poor into equality. Then there's the entrepreneurial types who recognize this growing problem and come up with crazy products in trying to provide a solution. One company has a product out called Thumb Bands. These are small brightly colored rubber bands wide enough to have the message TXTNG KILLS imprinted on them. Supposedly, a reminder to the asshole texting and driving that this is not a wise choice. I cannot, however, state any sort of surprise on my part that the thumb bands are a hit. On the website Textingthumbbands.com, they have not only introduced new colors and messages on the original thumb bands but they have also added reminder bands for your wrists, bands that go directly on your device, and even bumper stickers and T-shirts. Again, damn I love conscious-free market capitalism. At least someone is benefiting from this bad habit of texting junkies.

There's another product on the market trying to make a difference called Thumb Socks. These are little colored booty-looking things you wear on your thumbs while you're driving your car, hopefully killing your craving to tap away on your device until you reach your destination. Their motto is, *When You Wear the Socks the Texting Stops.* Yeah, right. I can pretty much guarantee there's some savvy marketer out there right now getting ready to launch a product of golf-ball-sized foam rubber balls to wear on your thumbs while driving that would make it impossible to text on your device without removing the balls. Of course, this is really not an answer either. That would be kind of like trying to cure alcoholism by inventing the mouth cork. Not going to happen. The reality of this situation should be obvious. As long as there are texting devices and automobiles, there will always be some idiot who will be texting and driving. That's a given. Just like there's always been some idiot driving drunk ever since there have been automobiles and booze. There is nothing, and I mean nothing, that we can do to help these unfortunate folks. But that doesn't mean that you can't help yourself. Look out for these morons, keep your awareness keen, and do the best you can to save yourself from experiencing a horrible accident just because someone has his or her attention, face, and thumbs plastered on a device while behind the wheel.

It appears that as of mid-2013 the medical community in the United States, especially in the field of psychology, is beginning to recognize and offer treatment for hard-core texting junkies. They are even redefining various parts of the addiction in some pretty amazing ways. It's obvious that texting while driving is dangerous, but how about texting while sleeping? Seriously, I can't make this shit up. I don't need to. But I must admit to you this one had me groaning and shaking my head. According to Paula Ebben of CBS Boston:

> Everyone knows texting and driving is a bad idea, but now doctors have a new warning when it comes to our smartphones. More people are seeking help because they now find themselves texting while they are sleeping.
>
> Megan is one of those people. She admits she is hooked on all kinds of social media but was surprised to find she was sending texts in the middle of the night that she didn't remember the next day.

"I guess I got up and texted and went back to bed, but I don't remember it," said Megan. "Four o'clock in the morning, three o'clock in the morning—it would just be sentences of jumbled up stuff."

Dr. Joseph Warburg, a sleep expert, said, "Technology has infiltrated the bedroom. The bedroom should really be a very low-tech place."

Doctors are reporting more cases of so-called "sleep texting." Although there is obvious potential for embarrassment, there is also a concern about the health consequences.

"They are not getting the deep sleep, or the rapid eye movement sleep, which is really critical to higher brain functions," explained Dr. Werber.

Laura Hogya is also a sleep texter. "I wake up exhausted the next day, and I don't know if it is from tossing and turning or answering a text message."

Dr. Werber says the first step to take to break this cycle is obvious: move the phone out of the bedroom. That's what Megan has done. "Sometimes I will put it here in my vanity, and other times if I'm really stressed out, I'll keep it all the way out here," she said as she pointed to a table down the hallway.

In general Dr. Werber believes it is a good idea to remove all gadgets from the bedroom to ensure a good nights sleep. "The light is also disturbing your ability to go to sleep because it's sending a signal to your brain that you still want to be awake."

Gee, do you think. What's the next step here? Possibly a texting pillow?

All right, we're almost finished. Let me see if I can sum this thing up in a reasonable fashion within the next couple of pages. And if you feel there should be a different conclusion to the book, please let me know on the book's website.

www.deadguyonfacebook.com

Conclusion

At times I may have come across in this book as an anti-technology, cranky old fart. This, however, is certainly not the case. I'm old enough to realize that in the big picture, we are still in the early dawn of computer technology. I'm also wise enough to realize that usage will continue to rise and the technology will continue to evolve. In other words none of this digital crap is going anywhere. Ever. Quite frankly I'm excited about this evolution of computer technology, and it thrills me when something comes along in the digital world that has a positive effect on my life. For example, nearly this entire book was written using the latest in voice recognition software. I love it. Wouldn't ever want to be without it again as much as I write. I am not annoyed with technology.

I frequently get annoyed with people who use and abuse it though. Yet my aggravation doesn't really last long, but my concern for them does. Are they being robbed of a full and vibrant life because of their addiction to their devices? Are they disconnecting from the real world because their main focus is firmly fixed in the digital one? Are they alienating human contact with friends and loved ones because the majority of the contact received by them is not in person? And will all this digital dicking around wind up having a negative effect on them physically, mentally, and spiritually? Are their devices doing more computing than the six inches of real estate between their ears? Likely the answer to many of these questions, if not all of them, is yes. But there is hope.

Some have said the proliferation of our digital world is causing a collapse in our social community. While I cannot completely disagree with this statement, I do not feel it's entirely accurate. I say this because our social tenets have been in rapid decline for decades, years before the digital dominance. Especially engagement in political, civic, religious, and community service activities. This lack of participation in social community even carries over to activities such as dinner parties and bowling leagues. In other words we are dropping out of our social networks, the face-to-face ones, at an alarming rate. While our digital addictions do not seem to be a big part of the cause of why this is happening, could there be a possibility that our digital devices could provide possible solutions to a revival of our social community? I believe they could. Reviving and rebuilding our social community requires that we transcend our professional and political and social identities to connect with people unlike ourselves. Our digital devices provide this connection like none other. Identifying with others instantly and digitally.

I believe it was my generation, the baby boomers, that was the guilty one, that began to collapse our sense of social community and civic obligation. I also believe the younger generations, the ones digitally connected or addicted, can begin to reverse this collapse through the proper use of their devices. After all, we live in a time where people should be ashamed and furious over the fact that their neighbors cannot locate employment that pays a living wage. A world where children still go to bed hungry and sick. A place where our elected leaders are more barbaric than Attila the Hun and kill innocent people around the world daily. A time when having meaningful conversations about how we can take better care of one another as fellow human beings is all but lost. Shouldn't all of this digital connectedness be utilized to its fullest, helping to make this earth a better place to live? I'm confident it can, and I hope and pray that it will be.

I could not end this book with any more fitting words than those of Nicholas Carr, best-selling author of the book *The Shallows: What the Internet Is Doing to Our Brains*. In his Pulitzer Prize finalist best selling book Carr states the following:

> People seem to be looking for ways to loosen technology's grip on their lives and thoughts. I saw signs of this backlash in the correspondence I received from readers of *The Shallows*. (Most of the notes arrived via e-mail, though I do have a sizable stack of typed and handwritten letters on my desk.) Dozens of people wrote to share their stories of how the web has scattered their attention, parched their memories, or turned them into compulsive nibblers of info-snacks. I was particularly struck by the large number of notes that came from young people—high schoolers, college kids, twentysomethings. They fear that constant connectivity may be constricting rather than expanding their horizons. Some of their stories are poignant. One college senior sent me a long e-mail describing how he has struggled "with a moderate to major form of Internet addiction since the third grade. I am unable to focus on anything in a deep and detailed manner," he wrote. "The only thing my mind can do, indeed the only thing it wants to do, is plug back into that distracted, frenzied blitz of online information." He is drawn back into the web even though he knows that "the happiest and most fulfilling times of my life have all involved a prolonged separation from the Internet."

I've always been suspicious of those who seek to describe the effects of digital media in generational terms, drawing sharp contrasts between young "Internet natives" and old "Internet immigrants." Such distinctions strike me as misleading, if not specious. If you look at statistics on web use over the past two decades, you see that the average adult has spent more time online than the average kid. Parents are as besotted with their BlackBerrys as their children are with their Xboxes. And the idea that those who grow up peering at screens will somehow manage to avoid the cognitive toll exacted by multitasking and persistent interruptions is a fantasy contradicted by neuroscientific research. All of us, young and old alike, have similar neutrons and synapses, and our brains are affected in similar ways by the media we use.

Net culture isn't youth culture; it's mainstream culture. And my guess is that if the incipient Net backlash expands into a broad movement, the people leading it will be not the nostalgic old but the idealistic young. It's worth remembering that one of the original targets of the sixties counterculture was the then-new mainframe computer, which seemed to be reducing human beings to strings of numbers. Campus protesters didn't just burn draft cards; they folded, spindled, and mutilated IBM punch cards. "Punch cards, used for class registration, were first and foremost a symbol of uniformity," the historian Steven Lubar has written, and "they became the symbolic point of attack."

Those times, and those attitudes, feel like ancient history now. As computers shrank, they became a lot less threatening. Eager for their assistance, we welcomed them into our homes and then into our pockets. But the young are still the enemies of uniformity, and the Internet, as it extends its reach into all the nooks and crannies of our days, is looking more and more like an enormous conduit of conventionality. What are Facebook and Google but giant institutions, arms of the new establishment? What are smartphones if not high-tech leashes? Today, online databases hold more information about us than could fit on a mile-high stack of punch cards. Some kind of rebellion seems in order.

Of course, in conjuring up a big anti-Net backlash, I may be indulging in a fantasy of my own. After all, the Internet tide continues to swell. In the months since I completed *The Shallows*, Facebook membership has doubled from 300 million to 600 million; the number of text messages processed each month by the typical American teen has jumped from twenty-three hundred to thirty-three hundred; sales of e-readers, tablets, and smartphones has skyrocketed; app stores have proliferated; elementary schools have rushed to put iPads in their students' hands; and the time we spend in front of screens has continued its seemingly inexorable rise. We may be wary of what our devices are doing to us, but we're using them more than ever. And yet history tells us, it's only against such powerful cultural currents that countercultural movements take place.

Thank you, Nicholas Carr, for your well-thought-out words of wisdom. If digital junkies begin to reawaken, and any sort of anti-Net backlash takes place in the future, the life-span of evil human-sized praying mantises may prove to be very short. Not that I feel in my heart this is really going to happen. Considering the rapid advance in nearly all digital technologies, I have to believe the digital junkie mentality is here to stay. Sure, there will always be a small minority that will choose to be in charge of its devices, yet the number of people whose devices are in charge of them will likely continue to grow. There's nothing you or I can do about that, but I would like you to consider putting yourself firmly in control of your digital life. You'd be amazed at the positive effect it can have on you.

I want to thank you for getting to the end with me on this digital mission. The book may be over, but my mission is not. If you enjoyed *Is It Safe to Friend a Dead Guy on Facebook* through humor, nonpolitically correct statements, or the silly reality of it all, I would appreciate you letting me know. You may do so on the website below, you can follow us on the Twitter feed @deadguyonfacebook, or you can even like us on Facebook. An honest review on Amazon is always appreciated. If you did not care for the book but just stuck it out until the end because of some twisted masochistic streak in you, I would also like to know. Call me out; tell me where I'm full of crap. I would appreciate your point of view, but don't think, for one minute, it will change mine. By the way, in case you're curious, I never did friend the dead guy on Facebook. I am, however, filled with gratefulness, and I thank Mr. Craig Rabiner for playing an important but posthumous role in this book.

www.deadguyonfacebook.com
#DGOFB

Author Biography

Steve Krupnik began his entrepreneurial life when he secured his first newspaper delivery route as an eight-year-old. He is an author, publisher, and business coach who has built, bought, and sold numerous businesses during his career. He is now the leading consultant in his business niche, and he writes and develops workbooks, audio courses, coaching programs, and informational videos and newsletters for businesses in various industries. He feels that his life experience has made him an expert at observing humankind and human nature.

Krupnik lives with his family in Indiana's South Bend area.